for my grandchildren
and future generations

Willie and Sandy Scott

HERD LADDIE
O THE GLEN
Songs of a Border Shepherd

WILLIE SCOTT
LIDDESDALE SHEPHERD AND SINGER

Introduction by Hamish Henderson
Compiled and Edited by Alison McMorland

This publication has been supported by

Graphic design and typesetting by Scottish Borders Council arts development

copyright © Alison McMorland and Scottish Borders Council 2006

contact: Scottish Borders Council arts development
Library HQ
St Mary's Mill
SELKIRK TD7 5EW
tel. 01750 724901
e-mail:ArtService@scotborders.gov.uk

ISBN 0-9545052-8-X

CONTENTS

ACKNOWLEDGEMENTS

This collection of songs was first published in June 1988. Eleven months later Willie Scott died on April 29th. He was coming up to his ninety second birthday. Ten years earlier in response to Willie's wish to have his songs written down in book form because 'People are aye askin me for the words o ma sangs' I had agreed to be his scribe; but it had taken much longer than expected. However a concentrated effort on my part to see it through coincided with the launch of an Appeal Fund in 1987 for The School of Scottish Studies at the University of Edinburgh. Finding ourselves unable to raise funding from the Scottish Arts Council or various Borders businesses in order to publish, Willie decided to fund the publication himself. We agreed that after costs had been covered the proceeds of the sale of the book should go to the Appeal Fund in recognition of the long association Willie had had with the SSS and in my case the personal help and encouragement I had been shown, especially from Hamish Henderson.

In the preparation of the book's first edition I received much help and again I wish to acknowledge this. From staff of the School of Scottish Studies ~ a body of people who wholeheartedly supported Willie's wish and respected his importance as a major traditional singer of the 20th century ~ Peter Cooke and Hamish Henderson both gave most generously in pre and post production advice and effort; Peggy Morrison for typing texts and Ian MacKenzie for preparation of photographs. There was kind hospitality from the Scott family, Sandy and Christine, Jim and Betty; and Matron and Mr Carlton of Weens House, Bonchester Bridge. Invaluable background information, keeping me right, was given by Jim and Sandy. Jean Beckhoffer helped with tape transcripts and my own family was most supportive; Dick; Anna and Ian. There was also interest and assistance from Rosie Capper, Curator of Hawick Museum and Richard White, also of Hawick Museum, who prepared map drawing and contributed his knowledge of the area. The music transcriptions of the songs were faithfully and skilfully carried out by Lance Whitehead.

We were grateful to receive permission for the reproduction of copyright photographs: front cover from the Scottish Daily Record & Sunday Mail; back cover photo from the School of Scottish Studies Archives; Copshawholm Fair, street scenes of old Hawick and Nine Stane Rig from Hawick Museum; Hermitage Castle from the Royal Commission on Ancient Monuments, Scotland; Willie Scott stick dressing at the Game Fair, Raby Castle, Co Durham from John Tarlton; Willie Scott carving crooks at Upper Monynut on the borders of East Lothian from the ' Farmers Weekly'. All other photos from Willie Scott's collection which included a detail of the Shepherd's Tartan, the family plaid: used as the cover background.

In this revised edition, I have taken the opportunity to give additional songs and transcripts, add song notes and make amendments. I am indebted to Geordie McIntyre for writing the song notes and his unfailing support. Again, I wish to thank the Scott family and, in particular Sandy, whose selfless enthusiasm helped to make this new edition possible. To Christine and Sandy, thank you for your friendship. To Dougie ~ who sadly died before its completion ~ and Cynthia, for shared times in remembering Willie. I should also like to thank Caroline Pugh for typing assistance; Lori Watson and Ian Abernethy for reproducing the hand written music on Sibellius; to Jo Miller for her advice on this and the final proof reading of the manuscript; additional photos from Sandy Scott; to Vic Smith for photos of Daisy Chapman and Geordie McIntyre for photo of Hamish Henderson. A special thank you to Iain Macaulay of Scottish Borders Council for his sustained commitment and support to this publication in recognition of Willie Scott's important tradition bearing status.

I should like to thank Dr Margaret McKay, Director of the School of Scottish Studies Archive, Edinburgh University, for encouragement and permission to include the Introduction by Hamish Henderson, originally published in Tocher, and for the assistance again given by Ian McKenzie in preparation of photographs. Finally, a thank you to the School of Scottish Studies for permission to use important material from the archives.

Alison McMorland

Notes on the editing of texts and music transcriptions

This collection of songs was initially selected by Willie Scott and myself. During this process I drew on my own personal recordings; Willie's manuscript copies of various songs; and the recordings undertaken by members of the School of Scottish Studies at the University of Edinburgh spanning over thirty years. The first of these recordings were undertaken by Francis Collinson in 1953, to be followed by Hamish Henderson and later by Ailie Munro. As well as songs, the bulk of my recordings concentrated on a shepherd's way of life; working and bringing up a family in the Liddesdale area. These are now precious memories, given by Willie at the end of his long, long life; however I only give a few accounts to illustrate the importance of his family's tradition of song and music -making and his memories of shepherding.

In transcribing song texts and the spoken word from tapes, I have tried to convey the flavour of the sung and spoken word through (in some cases) phonetic spelling; needless to say it remains a pale shadow of the live deliverance but in all cases remains true to the original.

A McMorland

While the melodies presented here are transcribed from particular performances they do not attempt to describe in detail all the subtle rythms of his renderings. Metronome markings indicate the approximate tempo of each song. For example the opening phrase of Jock Geddes and the Soo, sung in deliberate slow strathspey style by Willie Scott, would appear as follows if one attempted to show duration of notes with any real precision:

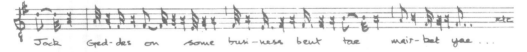

Nevertheless the freedom with which metre is treated by Willie's unaccompanied singing made it advisable to omit standard time signatures and a rigid form of barring, especially at the ends of phrases. Where particular rhythmic features are used in one verse only, they are placed within [ ]. Breath marks are denoted by apostrophes. Readers should also note that the "key signature" does not necessarily denote the tonality of the melody. This is especially true of hexatonic and pentatonic tunes such as *The Kielder Hunt*. The frequent glissandi used by the singer are indicated with oblique lines, eg the last line of *Callieburn*. Most songs have been transposed in pitch to avoid excessive use of leger lines and accidentals. Notes sharpened or flattened by nearly a quarter tone are shown by special characters, e.g. in the Wag at the Waa. Tenuto marks (-) show where a note is slightly lengthened.

Lance Whitehead

BIOGRAPHY ALISON MCMORLAND

Alison McMorland was born in Renfrewshire and has had a long involvement in the traditional arts on various levels: singer, collector, broadcaster, author and latterly tutor of Scots song in the Department of Scottish Music at Glasgow's RSAMD.

She came to wider public notice in the 1970s through her recordings and published song collections for Ward Lock Educational. Active in developing innovative projects, Alison later co-founded a community arts organisation, working primarily in this area for fifteen years whilst contributing to the Arts For Health movement in Scotland.

However songs and singing have been and remain at the very heart of what she is about. Under the inspirational guidance of the late Hamish Henderson who said, "Alison stands out as one of the principal modern interpreters of a ballad singing tradition ... uniting scrupulous traditional fidelity with versatile and resourceful creative artistry", she learned from some of the great traditional singers and, in particular, Willie Scott.

Since 2001 she has recorded a solo album, 'Cloudberry Day' and, in partnership with Geordie McIntyre, two CDs: 'Rowan in the Rock - songs of love, land and nature' and 'Ballad Tree - classic Scots ballads'. All three CDs are on the Living Tradition label. Alison is currently working with Elizabeth Stewart documenting the famed North - East traveller family: the Stewarts of Fetterangus.

INTRODUCTION
by
Hamish Henderson

In October 1961 the Howff Folk Song Club in Dunfermline held its first meeting. John Watt, the founder and organiser, had a promising corps of locals lined up, and he had invited several performers from the "parent" Howff in the High Street of Edinburgh, but the man who stole the show at that memorable opening night was neither Fifer nor Edinburgher. He was a tall, slowspoken silver-haired shepherd from the Borders, sixty-four years old at that time, who was employed at Kingseat of Outh, above Kelty, and had come along after hearing that the Club was starting and that there was a seat reserved for him.

When Willie Scott rose to sing that evening he was well aware that the audience of youthful folk fans gathered in the smoky room was probably not too familiar with the sound of traditional Scots folk song. Furthermore, there was always a possibility - seeing that the Howff was a completely new venture - that one or two of the younger ones might be tempted to "take the mickey". Any fears of this sort were instantly dispelled when Willie started singing. He struck up *There's Bound to be a Row* with easy confidence and confiding drollery, and it was clear

Singing in Dunfermline at the Howff Folksong club in 1961. The founder and organiser of the Club, John Watt, is sitting to the right of Willie Scott.

before he had come to the end of the song that he had completely won over this new audience.

In previous years Willie had, of course, performed hundreds of times at herds' suppers and at the Border kirns, to audiences sharing his own background, predilections and speech idioms. His father - also a shepherd - had been a singer, and Willie remembers well the jollifications at fairs and sales all over the Border country when he was a child.

> There was aye singin at the clippins, and at night the fiddle would come oot and they'd start dancin.

The same pattern of life continued, with very little change, throughout his working career, and the Scottish revival folk scene was therefore lucky to become the beneficiary of a tradition so vital, and yet so solid and homogeneous. At Dunfermline the world of John Leyden and James Hogg seemed to communicate directly with the new cosmopolitan folk audience of industrial Scotland through the lips and personality of this masterly veteran tradition-bearer.

William James Scott, scion of a long line of Border shepherds, was born at Andrew's Knowes in the Dumfriesshire parish of Canonbie on 7th May 1897; his father was working there at the time as a game-keeper. Canonbie is just about as near the Border as you can get in that area, so Willie was born a Scotsman by an even narrower margin than Hugh MacDiarmid (a native of Langholm three or four miles to the north). He was one of a family of seven children, nearly all of whom turned out to be gifted singers and musicians - particularly his elder brother Tom whose voice can be heard on the Folkways LP 'The Borders' (FW 8776). Tom (who died on 21st April 1970) was also a versatile performer on fiddle, accordion, `moothie' and Jew's harp. When he was a wee loon, Willie taught himself to play the fiddle, and a love for traditional Lallan folk music - particularly the dance tunes - has remained with him throughout his life.

As Willie's father took a job across the Border in Cumberland just after the turn of the century, Willie got his first schooling near Brampton, so he early became acquainted with the lore of the "land of the beck" as well as with that of the "land of the burn". (It is noteworthy that two of his most popular items *Irthingwater Hounds* and *The Kielder Hunt* are songs from the English side.) After three years, however, his father was back in Scotland, and Willie got the rest of his schooling at Ewes, near Langholm, and later at Allanwater, in the parish of Teviothead.

Willie left school at eleven years of age to start work on a farm at Stobbs near Hawick. He worked a twelve hour day from 6 a.m. to 6 p.m. (or later, if you could still see). For these long hours of farm service he received seven shillings (35p) a week - which was all that was left of his wage after the cost of his keep had been deducted. Willie stayed at Stobbs until he was sixteen; he then accompanied his father to Northhouse, Allerybar, Teviotdale, where he did the same work (general farm service) until he was eighteen.

Willie Scott married when he was nearing twenty; his bride was Frances Isabel Thomson, the daughter of a Canonbie ploughman. The wedding took place on the 13th April 1917 at Almondside, Canonbie. Frances was a champion whistler, who won every whistling competition on the west marches of the Border; she was also a good singer - Willie learnt his version of *The Bonnie Wee Tramping Lass* from her - and no mean accordionist. In addition, she was fond - like Willie himself - of taking part in amateur dramatics; Frances and he appeared together in one of Joe Corrie's plays. They had six children, all of whom to a greater or lesser extent inherited their parents' musical talents. Willie and his wife were together for forty-three years; she died on June 10th 1960.

Willie Scott's life from 1917 until his retirement in 1969 was very much the life described in *The Shepherd's Song* (which latter, incidentally, he first heard old Willie Graham of

Gorrenberry sing "at the dippin" when just a boy at school). Not long after his marriage he went to Dryhope in what he himself calls the "Hogg" country; he herded at the Hirsel, two miles up St. Mary's Loch. After a year at Dryhope he moved to Braidlie, near Hermitage Castle, and remained there for nine years. His longest stay in one place was during his next engagement, at the Nine Stane Rig (where the famous warlock Lord Soulis was boiled); here he remained for sixteen years. Following this he shepherded at Hartwoodmyres which is in the Ettrick valley, staying there for nine years. It was during this period that Francis Collinson discovered and recorded Willie and his elder brother Tom for the School of Scottish Studies.

Here is Frank Collinson's own account of how he got to know Willie:

> It was in the early 1950s that I first heard of him. I was in fact about to make my first survey as a member of the newly formed School of Scottish Studies of the possibility of collecting folk-songs and ballads anew in the Borders. I knew well Sir Walter Scott's Minstrelsy of the Scottish Border, but that was made over a hundred years ago. I myself had known the Borders since boyhood; but I had never come across any folk-singing - the folk music in the farm cottages and bothies was all performed on the button accordion - (and that with great skill!). It seemed that the flood of song of Scott's day, of the riding ballads and the great romantic and historical ballads of the Border had dwindled to a trickle in these later times.
>
> In my new approach to the subject, Willie Scott was the first name that came my way - and that from more than one informant. I was living in Melrose, in `The kindly house of Huntlyburn' of Scott's Diaries; and it was there that I heard of him. He was then the shepherd at the 'out-bye' farm of Hartwoodmyres in Selkirkshire, about ten miles from where I lived. Hartwoodmyres is one of the high-lying sheep-farms of the country to the south-west of Selkirk, in the heart of the old Ettrick Forest, a hill-pasture country of single-track roads with numerous farm gates across them, all requiring to be opened and shut by the motorist on his way there. The countryside around was redolent of Border ballad titles; Dodhead, (*Whae's this brings the fraye to me?*); Carterhaugh of the ballad of *Tamlane*; Yarrow of *O Willie's Rare and Willie's Fair*; the Douglas Burn of *The Douglas Tragedy*; and for good measure, Deloraine of Sir Walter Scott's *Lay of the Last Minstrel* - all at no great distance.
>
> I found Willie Scott at the farm and received the warm welcome that, as I came to know, is characteristic of him. There was no electricity at the farm in those days for mains-driven recording machines, but I possessed a clock-work driven 'Reporter' machine that had served me well in recording Gaelic songs in the Highlands, and this was good enough for a preliminary survey. The first song Willie sang for me was *The Shepherd's Song* - "I can smear my sheep and dip," with a tune consisting of a single repeated Dorian phrase. His next was *Sweet Copshawholm* (the old name for Newcastleton); then *Irthing Water Foxhounds* and *The Kielder Hunt* a grand song!
>
> Soon afterwards I had another session with Willie and other members of his family whom he had brought along with him, at Bonchester Bridge. Here there was electricity, and having brought with me our technician from the School, James ("Tony") Anthony, we were able to make better recordings of the songs he had sung before, and to record others which

he had remembered since. The new songs included *Jimmie Raeburn, The Lads that were Reared among Heather, Farewell to the Borders*, and of course, *The Tinker's Weddin*.

Soon afterwards Willie moved to Hawick, and further recordings followed.

Later still, he moved to Fife, and I lost touch with him for a number of years. When I met him again he was singing at folk- song concerts, and was well on his way to becoming a folksong celebrity on radio and television.

Willie has since greatly increased the repertoire of songs from the bountiful recesses of his memory, to the point where he can be reckoned as a major contributor to our present-day knowledge of the songs and lore of the Borders.

To me, one of the most interesting of his recollections are two verses and the tune of the old Border riding ballad of *Jamie Telfer of the Fair Dodhead*. I never expected this to turn up at such a late date, and I will always regret that it did not fall to me to record it.

Frank Collinson wrote out these reminiscences in 1981, not long before his own death, and it is a source of real satisfaction to us that we are able to include them in the present introduction.

After leaving Hartwoodmyres, Willie moved out of the Borders for the first time; as Frank records, he went to Kingseat of Outh, which is in the Cleish Hills above Kelty, and he remained there for nearly eleven years. It was while he was there that he underwent his baptism of fire as a traditional singer in folk clubs - it was at the Howff in Dunfermline, as described in the first paragraphs above.

In November 1963 he moved to Upper Monynut, on the borders of East Lothian and Berwickshire, and stayed there until his retirement in November 1968. His subsequent career brought him many further moves, including trips as far afield as the USA and Australia.

About the shepherd's life there is no space to write here: readers are referred to R. B. Robertson's "Of Sheep and Man" (London 1944). However, it may not be out of place to remind readers that there can be few professions which call for such self-abnegating devotion to one's charges as that of a shepherd. One single story - not from Willie, although he has his own memories of shepherds who perished in the snow - must serve to remind us of this easily forgotten fact. On 6th May 1956 the Sunday Mail carried a story about a seventeen-year-old shepherd, Ralph Forlow, who loved his sheep and died for them in 1954, in a blizzard high up in the Galloway hills. A search party found him days later lying dead in the shelter of a wall; the howls of his faithful collie had guided them to where it stood over the body. A memorial cairn was erected at the foot of Millfire, where the boy died: on a tablet set in the cairn are the following lines:

> On Scotland's page o' gilded fame
> Inscribe the shepherd hero's name,
> Gie him a place amang the great

> The men o' war, or kirk or state,
>
> An' add this message, chiselled deep;
>
> "The guid herd died tae save his sheep."

There is another old saying, which Willie would no doubt endorse: "Ony fule can write a book, but it taks a man tae herd the Merrick".

After Willie's entree to the folk scene via John Watt's Howff in Dunfermline, he became almost a resident singer at this establishment. Then things moved very fast indeed. Bruce Dunnet (who was working for Arnold Wesker's Centre 42) invited him to appear at the Singers' Club in London in November 1961; thereafter he was continually receiving invitations from all over Britain. He appeared at the traditional folk music get-togethers at Keele and Loughborough; got invitations to Edinburgh and Glasgow, and to Whitby, Redcar, Girvan and many other festivals, rapidly becoming one of the best-known figures in the entire revival. When the Blairgowrie festivals, organised by the Traditional Music and Song Association of Scotland, began in the mid-sixties, he presented a cup for the Men's Traditional Singing and promptly carried it off himself. When "Blairgowrie" became Kinross, Willie stayed with it and helped to build up its nationwide popularity. New ventures such as the Keith Festival (first held in 1976) received his enthusiastic support, and on his own home ground he helped to make the Newcastleton Festival one of the most enjoyable events of the summer Folk season.

As many who have followed his career in the Revival can confirm, his involvement with the "new wave" of singers and musicians has been by no means solely a one-way process. If hundreds of young folk benefitted greatly from making his acquaintance and hearing him

Willie with, on his right, Pat McNulty the Irish piper and on his left hand side, Davie Stewart and Jimmy MacBeath: Blairgowrie Festival 1968, organised by the Traditional Music, Song Association of Scotland.

sing, he too drew a great deal of sustenance and inspiration from this ever-widening folk scene. It also gave him an opportunity which he might otherwise not have had of meeting a number of traditional singers from widely differing parts of Scotland. What could happen in this maelstrom of creativity and community experience is vividly illustrated by the development, on Willie's lips, of the Kintyre song *Callieburn* (*Machrihanish Bright and Bonnie*). This song, which refers to an emigration from Kintyre in the early nineteenth century, was preserved in the repertoire of the MacShannon family in and around Machrihanish: I first heard it from the late James MacShannon (also a shepherd) in 1940. Eighteen years later Willie Mitchell, a butcher from Campbeltown, recorded it for the School of Scottish Studies; he sang a longer version which he had collected from Mr. Reid, the farmer at Callieburn. At this same session in 1958 Alec MacShannon recorded the short version preserved in his family.

For several years I had tried to get Willie Mitchell to come with members of his family to one or other of the folk music events of the period; eventually he turned up at the Blairgowrie Festival of 1968, and the scene was set for a creative fusion of considerable interest.

Willie Scott takes up the tale:

> It was ae night in the Sun Lounge of the Angus Hotel. It was one of the best parties I've ever been at. I'd never met Willie Mitchell - I never kent there was such a man. He stole the show earlier on at the Men's Singing. I asked him for songs I'd hear from shepherds at the ram sales. . right back. . and I ca'd him Mr. Mitchell. He said, 'Dinna put handles to my name - nae misters. I'm just Willie Mitchell'. 'Weel', I said, 'I enjoyed you. Hearin you in the hall - *Nancy's Whisky* - made my festival.' (He enjoyed meetin' us people too. I got letters showing how pleased he was).

This impromptu "ceilidh" in the Sun Lounge of the Angus will remain life-long in the memory of everyone who was there. Archie Fisher gave of his best, and several other people sang, but Willie Scott demanded more songs from Willie Mitchell, and eventually he sang Callieburn using the tune already recorded from the MacShannons; his daughter and son-in-law joined in. Willie Scot was tremendously struck by the song, asked later for it to be sung again, and got Willie Mitchell to write out the words. A few months later I recorded him singing it. The words were as he had received them from Willie Mitchell, but the tune had been totally transformed. For me - and I'm sure for all the others who were there - the midnight ceilidh in the Sun Lounge of the Angus marked a real moment of qualitative break-through - tradition and revival, working together, had actually made it! As the late Arthur Argo once put it: if all our efforts in the Folk Revival were now to drain away into the sands, it would have been worth it for that midnight ceilidh.

Willie has often taken shepherds' crooks carved by himself to the various festivals he has attended, and those who have seen them will acknowledge that in this sphere too he is both craftsman and artist. He has received many prizes for his outstandingly beautiful crooks and, in 1953, he was commissioned by the Borders Stick Dressers Association to make sticks for the Queen and Duke of Edinburgh. He was introduced to the Queen on their presentation. For years he has been a familiar figure at the Highland Show at Ingliston, exhibiting his produce.

In October 1969 Willie was admitted to Peel Hospital, Galashiels, and underwent a major operation. He was kept in hospital for six months, but thereafter made a very successful recovery.

It remains to add that Willie's children and grandchildren are carrying on the tradition of the singing Scotts. Sandy and Jim are excellent singers, and Dougie sings and plays the accordion. Willie's grandson Lindsay - the son of Robert, who died eleven years ago - is one of the "wild rovers of the Revival". The son whom Willie regarded as the best singer of the lot - Thomas - was killed over Holland on New Year's Day 1945 while serving with the RAF. He is buried at Cleves.

In March 1977 the Edinburgh Folk Club, then domiciled at 23 George Square, paid a friendly visit to the Hawick Folk Club, where they were received by Willie Scott. Willie liked the look of the Sandy Bell's Broadsheet T-shirt and expressed a wish to acquire one. But there was one snag, "The trouble wi thae T-sarks," he said, "is they're ower smaa."

A crook and a T-sark! This seems a fitting escutcheon for Hawick's Will Scott, whom we greet with affection, admiration and gratitude on the eve of his ninety-first birthday.

Hamish Henderson
June 1988

stages of stick-dressing

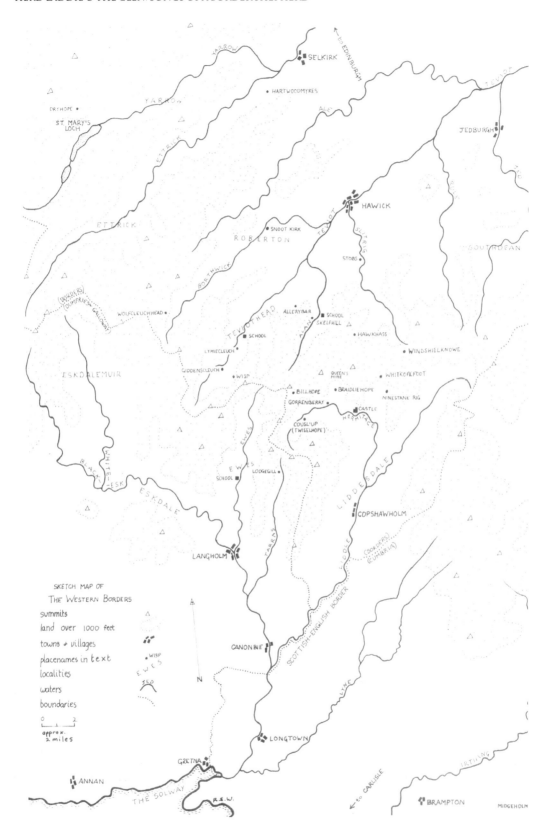

SKETCH MAP OF
THE WESTERN BORDERS

summits

land over 1000 feet

towns & villages

placenames in text

localities

waters

boundaries

Locations showing the areas Willie Scott lived and worked in the Borders

Born **1897** at **Andrew's Knowes, Canonbie**.

The Scott family moved to **Haining House** at **Brampton** and in **1902** Willie attended school at **Midgeholm**.

The Scott family moved to **Lodgegill** where he went to **Ewes** school.

Family moved to **Gideonscleugh** where he went to **Teviothead** school.

1903 (approx)the family moved to **Hawkhass** where Willie attended school at **Allanwater, Teviothead**.

1909-10 left school when he was coming up to the age of 12 years. The family was there 9 years altogether, living within the vicinity of **The Queen's Mire.**

1913 Willie and his father took the positions of two herds: Willie did the man's job and his father did the boy's. They went to **Northhouse, Allerybar** in Teviotdale.

1917 - 1918 Willie Scott and Frances Thompson married at **Almondside, Canonbie** and on their marriage moved to **Dryhope** in the **Yarrow Valley.** Isabel, the first of their six children was born there

1918 - 1927 they moved to **Braidliehope** where their three sons, Jim, Robert and Thomas were born.The children attended **Hermitage** school passing daily the formidable **Hermitage Castle.** The many stories of this area included that of Lord Soulis as retold by Willie.

1927 - 1939 Windshielknowe where the two youngest sons, Sandy and Douglas, were born. The four older children attended **Riccarton Junction** school, a four mile walk over the hills.

1939 - 1944 The family moved on to **Whiteropefoot**, a farm owned by the same farmer as **Windeshielknowe** but on the main Hawick to Copshie road. Again they were near a historic site namely **Nine Stane Rig** (now under forestry).

1944 - 1953 Hartwoodmyres was the next settled place of employment in the **Ettrick** valley where the children went to school at **Ettrickbridge End** and **Selkirk.**

1953 –1963 Kingseat of Outh Willie and Frances moved out of the Borders for the first time to the Cleish hills above Kelty. It was here that Frances died in1960. While living in this area Willie had 'his baptism of fire as a traditional singer in folkclubs at the Howff in Dunfermline'.

1963 -1968 Upper Monynut on the borders of East Lothian and Berwickshire where he retired to **Hawick.**

1968 until his death in **1989** Willie lived in **Hawick**, latterly staying with his son Sandy and partner Christine Russell at St Boswells for two years. Up until this time he travelled widely to singing engagements at clubs and festivals all over Britain,and further afield to Australia and the States. Ambassador of Border song and lore, he was much loved , appreciated and respected by all who knew him within the folksong world.

Whiteropefoot Farm

and Lambs Sold well at
the market
During the years I was there
we had some storms but
did not last long but
the winter of 1963 fit to days
before Christmas and I never
saw the Post man till the
21st of March had nothing but
hay and the had never been
hayed befor and they eat
it right away snow was
very deep and hard frozen
it was a very bad winter for
stock of any kind it was very
wind swept and very open
to any dirt the wind was in
I left in November 1953 and
went to Upper Monyknut in
East Lothian it was long road

Extract from Willie's own written account of events in his life.

WILLIE SCOTT
Song Sources and
Reflections on Shepherding

Alison McMorland working with Willie on his collection of songs
for publication in 1988.

Willie Scott's very early introduction to songs was from his parents and in particular his mother Ellen Telfer. Although both his parents sang, it was from her that he learnt songs he was to sing all his life. Before marrying James Scott she had been a farmhouse cook and one time servant at Hermitage Castle farm . Ellen had a fine sense of the history of the area and in songs that reflected life's struggles, of which they had had their fair share; while Willie's father was considered the 'best read shepherd in the area' with a deep love of Burns's songs and poems; and of Leyden and Hogg, the Ettrick Shepherd. Willie's account of how he first heard his mother sing *Jimmie Telfer o the Fair Dodheid* captures his boyhood days.

Jim and Ellen Scott with five of their seven children:(from left to right) cousin Nell, Jock, Sandy, Mat ,Willie and Cis. Taken at Hawkhass about 1913.

> Sherrif Boyd at Jedburgh wis riding wi a cavalcade over the way Mary Queen o Scots rode to visit Bothwell in Hermitage Castle, an A got the day off the school for tae show them the way owre the Queens Mire; an they gave me a gold soverign.
>
> It wes a dark, foggy day an…well A knew the way there right enough, but A'd never been the road frae the top o me father's hill down to this road. So A got them conveyed owre there an cam back up tae the Queen's Mire, tae whaur Mary Queen o Scots bogged her horse an lost her silver spur. A wes told tae keep tae the top o the ridge on the hill; an A came tae the corner of the fence that wes joining me father's hill, an A knew where A was then.
>
> Ma mither sang twae verses of *JimmieTelfer an the Fair Dodheid* . She sang them tae me because A wes chosen tae show them the way.

> Warn Wat o Harden an his sons
> And gar them ride Borthwick water wide;
> Warn Gowdielands an Allenhaugh
> An Gilmanscleuch an Commonside.
>
> As he passed the yetts of Priesthaughswire
> Tae warn the curious o the lea;
> An as he cum doon the Hermitage Slack
> Warn doughty Willie o Gorrenberry.

It's caad Priestshaughswire on the map, but we never caa it nocht but the Queen's Mire. What made it more interesting, when I wes at Braidliehope, a herded the Queen's Mire; aa the road frae the top doon intae Hermitage. A've drucken at the well at Hatternside an aa, Queen Mary's well they caa it. A've covered aa the road according tae *Jimmy Telfer's Fair Dodheid*; on foot, after dark and in the light.

Well the first time I heard ma mother and some o them singing of a night was when the clipping was finished; they'd mebbe be a gamekeeper who played the pipes and twae or three o the ald fermers that wes clippin that wid sing a song and they might hae a dance outside. She'd a variety o songs *The Dowie Dens O Yarrow, Come AA Ye Tramps and Hawkers, Jimmie Raeburn, Time Wears Awa, When Fortune Turns her Wheel, Pulling Hard Against The Stream, Copshawholm Fair, Twas On Yin Night in Sweet July* (also known as Brundenlaws) and *When the Kye Cam Hame*. There were others (not included here) *Burns and His Highland Mary, Sae Will We Yet*, the *Whiles O Weary, Queer Folk O The Shaw*. A mind ther wes an old saying in Ettrick aboot "the queer folk o the Shaws". Ma mither wes aye hummin an singin aroon the place, she knew a lot, mebbe juist a verse or twae like *Castles in the Air*:

> This world is all a bubble no matter where you go
> There's naething here but trouble, hardship, toil and woe;
> Go where you will, do what you may, you're never free frae care;
> And at its best this world is just castles in the air.

Aye I've seen her sing tae keep us devils quiet!

Willie vividly remembers the 'hill pairties' where such songs were shared:

It happened every winter, each person had a visitation; there were mebee twae families went each night an then the twae families cam tae your hoose. It wisnae juist every night ye know but it happened ther might be a fortnight atween them, mostly when the mune was full, so as ye could see tae come hame. The whole lot went, bairns an aa. The men were mebbe playin cards or draughts an some of the weemin brought their knitting. The lassies wouldna get a drink, but the men hed a dram. Whisky was only a shillun an the big bottles twae shilluns, but the weemen didn't drink much then.

If ther wes a young shepherd at the hoose, he cam with them an that's how the kinda sing –songs got a going. That's whaur ye got the sangs. If the young shepherd cam frae a far distance an he had a different song, if ee liked it ye'd memorise it at great length, an ee got roon aboot tae askin him tae gie ye the words o't. Ther wes hardly a hoose in them hill glens but had a fiddle or twae hingin in the hoose, an auld melodeon an yon Jewish harps. Ther wes hardly a body but could play somethin or sing a sang. Somebody would say " c'mon ye'll hae tae sing a sang," there it wes, an it juist kinda gaed roon with the lot.

At school the Dominie would lead a daily song session which would include: *Lock The Door Lariston, Dick Turpin And His Bonnie Black Bess, Scots Wha Hae, Sir Patrick Spens* and other songs. Recitation was also part of the curriculum and *Johnnie Armstrong* was recited around the class 'a verse apiece.'

When his brothers left home to work the circle widened and new song contacts were made.

> Me second brither Jock wes away up at Roberton, at a place caad Cleuchheid an A'd go up an see him, mebbe for a dance....sometimes they sorta gathert up at a little wee kirk place, the Snoot Kirk, doon at Deanburnhaaf (haugh) and they hed bits o sing-sangs. Well, ther wes an ald man Cherlie Scott had a kinda ald song schuil, his way on't. He learnt a lot o the young lads ald sangs, he likit hearin them. Roberton at that time wes a great singing country, every hoose in the valley knew aa these sangs. That ald Mr Scott wes a fermer, he nivver hed whisky in his mooth in his life.

Songs Willie learnt from his brother Jock were: *Bound To Be A Row, Donald's Return To Glencoe, Green Grows The Laurels, The Wild Colonial Boy* and *Johnny Raw.*

Songs learnt from his eldest brother Tom: *The Band O Shearers, Bloody Waterloo, Owre The Muir Amang The Heather* and *The Lads That Were Reared Amang Heather.*

Willie recalls that on the 14th of October 1914 , his brother Tom and his friend John Galbraith enlisted with the Gordon Highlanders. They were both working in the Rothbury area and returned home on foot and by train to say goodbye to their families.

> They walkit across tae oor place at Hawkhass,hed their denner an then they walkit oan tae Galashiels and listed an stayed wi his parents. They cam back an stayed aa nicht wi us. We hed a sing –song and John sang twae sangs: *Watchin The Wag At The Waa* and *Sons O Bonnie Scotland*; A thought it (*Sons O Bonnie Scotland*) wes a tremendous guid sang an got the words frae him. A sung it in the January at a charity concert for the Comfort Fund for the soldiers. John nivver cam back. He wes kilt. Ther wes a little lad away a guid while in the trenches, he got wounded an when he landed back he gave my cousin *The Soldier's Return*. Well they wur pals an ma cousin always sang twae sangs, *The Learig* and *The Whiles O Weary* ; ee says tae ma cousin "A've a new song for ee" and gave him what he'd composed in the trenches.

The pattern of life Willie was to know all his working days was established early in his childhood. The passing of the seasons intertwined with the shepherd's work of lambing, dipping , clipping and ram sales.

> Ther wes some gey warriors aboot et that time, but the warriors aboot aa deid. That's one thing 'at A've seen disappearing greatly, is dry humour wi herds. It wes fair the spice o life aboot clippin time, ragtaggin yin another.

It was on these occasions that he heard songs sung by old characters as Willie Graham of Gorrenberry. From him Willie learnt: *The Shepherd's Song, An Awfu Chap for Fun, John Reilly* and others.

The following list of singers from whom Willie learnt other songs could almost read as a guide to the Liddesdale area:

From Archie Thompson of Black Hall Ewes, *Jock Geddes An The Soo*;

Tom Elliot of Lymiecleuch of the Wisp Hills, *Killiebank Braes*;

Tommy Beatty of Cous'lup (Twiselhope) *Irthing Water Foxhounds* and *The Kielder Hunt*;

Wull Scott at Bilhope, *Piper McNeil*;

Jim Scott of Cranesleuch, Falstone Farm, *Bonnie Tyneside*;

Stanley Henry of Copshie (Newcastleton) *Lambing time*;

Other songs were learnt that were popular but not connected to one person: the *Soft Lowland Tongue O The Border*, *My Hielan Hame*, *Scotch Medley* and many more not included in this collection of songs but popular at the time.

During the winter months the Auld Year's Nicht celebrations gave the opportunity for singing, dancing and reciting. A faded photograph in Willie's possession catches one of these occasions.

Willie (centre front row) with the Guisers on Hogmanay 1924. A verse remembered from this occasion was:

**Rise up ald wife and shake yer feathers, dinna think that we are beggars;
When bairns gan oot tae play, rise up an gies oor Hogmanay.**

... taen at Gorenberry doon below Braidliehope whaur I lived up above Hermitage Castle. Up the water. We aa met at the gamekeeper's hoose first, his wes the lowest hoose in the top o the valley...an ther were a dram an ee got a bit cake, an sang a sang. Ye'd go mebee fifty or sixty yairds up an across the bridge an ee were received there. Well he wes ma boss, so he mostly gave us a bottle o whiskey away wi us. Then we went tae anither place an he'd gie us oor supper, pigeon pie. Ther were a lot o pigeons aboot the place an she always got them shot an made a big pie, o as big as a small table y'know. Ye got a pigeon apiece, the legs were stickin oot o the top o the crust. We were aa disguised an A sung in a Northumberland twang so's they widnae ken whae A wes; an A played the fiddle an the'd mebee do a Hielan Scottische or anything A'd a mind tae play they'd dance. The sang A sung wes *Bound Tae Be A Row* …. O A learnt that afore A left the schuil. A got it from me brither Jock. Ther wes a fella sang something aboot a lass that wes sweet nineteen an she gaed hame an screwed aff a hind

Taking a break while building peat stacks at Braidliehope in 1922. Frances and Willie with their children Isabella, Robert and Jim. Hillwalkers from Copshawholm (back row) took this early photo.

leg an took an eye oot….he should've been lyin oan the chair, she wesnae in bed wi him! *Mistress Paxton's Shop* wes a great favourite o Frances, ma wife, that was her pairty piece, that an *Bonnie Wee Trampin Lass* on Auld years Nicht.'

Also during the winter months were the Herds' Suppers:

The Shepherds' Suppers wur held onytime frae the end o Ocotber tae the end o January. One at Selkirk, one at Etterick, one at Peebles and one at Hawick an ee attended them aa. Ye gave the likes o the Duke o Buccleugh a complimentary ticket tae come an propose the toast tae Agriculture an mebbe Sir Francis a ticket if he'd come an propose a toast tae the Herds; well ye'd tae hev somebody tae reply so ee gave them a complimentary ticket.

Then ye'd tae have at least a couple o singers for tae come in between the toasts an reply tae the toast; song mebbe, one this time an one the next time. The thing finished aboot eeleven o'clock wi a special licence to one (o' clock); then the toffs gathered up an went away when aa the speechifying wis dune an the whole bunch got together for a ceilidh. Aa them that could sing hed a song tae sing. A sung a lot certainly, but ony function A went tae ther wes juist twae songs they wanted an it wes the twae hunting songs, *Kielder Hunt* an *Irthing Water Foxhounds*. There were other songs A'd have likit tae sing, but if it wes a

Displaying carpet bool trophies.

Shepherds' Dinner or owt like that, it had tae be that or ee widnae been asked.

Hunting - nae on horse back - but A've walkit mony a thoosan miles following the hunt. A've been right away up, o ten miles above Cowpsha , feenished up in Westerkirk an head hame tae come cross country. When A wes at Windshielknowe, A feenished way up almost at the top o the Carter. Aa the herds were on fit an juist the huntsmen, a matter o a couple following on horseback. It wis yer entertainment. If it wis a guid day ye could go ,but if it wis stormy an ye were needin tae be hame wi yer sheep, ye couldnae go. Hungry job tho'. When ye got sterted ye couldnae think o stopping if the thing wis going right ye know. Ye feenished miles frae hame an ye were as hungry as a bloody hawk. Ye took a bit piece in yer pocket, but ye always thocht ye'd be hame afore dennertime ken. The hunting feenished aboot the eleventh o April. Hunting and carpet bools wes the the only sport ye had. Aye ye were glad tae get away for a race, aboot twice a week.

At the Herds' Suppers my boss used tae dae *MacAlister* an A more or less just memorised it. A had a guid memory, the likes o *Bonnie Tyneside* and *Irthing Water Foxhounds*, ther wes only a matter o twae or three words A hadnae when A actually got the words. If A heard a song A thocht wis guid, aye a good air and a story attached to it…well A laid masel oot tae try an get it; because A could always min whit the air wes. One night a man recited *Sonny Snell* an the next morning at the rams sale Willie McFarlane an I got it completed by the time we'd sorted the tups oot fur the sale! A hed a tremendous amount o songs; a got them frae a fella Sanderson in Glesca. They were just preentit like newspapers, in columns an they just clippit oot what ye wanted; mebbe a penny for half a column; five verses a penny or if it wes a long thing mebbe thrupence. He sent a catalogue oot an ye juist wrote what the name o the song wes that ye wanted and sent the money away. O mebbe a matter o two bob …. average aboot tuppence apiece.

Over the years Willie set poems to traditional airs. Included in this collection are *Hermitage Castle*, arranged when he was living nearby at Braidliehope; *Fareweel Tae The Borders*, *The Yella Haired Laddie* and *Sweet Copshawholm*. The latter was written by James Telfer, one time schoolmaster at Saughtree school and a great uncle of Willie on his mother's side of the family.

From the early sixties onwards Willie's repertoire widened. Singing at festivals run by The Traditional Music and Song Association brought him into contact with singers from all over Scotland and a natural song exchange took place with new found friends.

He mixed with the likes of Davie Stewart, Jimmy McBeath and Willie Mitchell enjoying the banter and humour between them that was reminiscent of his earlier singing days with his cronies. Charlie Murray's rendition of the *Waddin O McPhee* (to the tune of *Loch Lomond*) became a firm favorite and was taken up by Willie.

At mony sprees I've been, but the best I've ever been

Was held high up on Ben Lomond;

Every yin got fu, it was like a Waterloo

At the waddin o McPhee on Ben Lomond.

Some cam up the high road , some cam up the low road,

An some o them got lost in the gloamin;

An them that bide awa, they wernae there at aa

At the waddin o McPhee on Ben Lomond.

Enjoying the company of Daisy Chapman of Aberdeen and various joint singing engagements, he learnt *Kissin In the Dark, Banks Of Inverurie* and *Bonnie Udney* ; from Willie Mitchell of Campbeltown, Argyll, he learnt *Nancy's Whiskey, Boys O Boys* and *Callieburn*; from Gus Russell *The Time O Year For Dippin Sheep* and from Pete Shepheard, the text of *The Banks of Newfoundland*. While on a singing trip with Jean Redpath to America, in Willie's own words he 'collected' *The Shepherds' Counting System* from Tom Rush, whose father had emigrated from Scotland in the late twenties.

Willie Scott with Daisy Chapman.

Willie Scott's collection of songs include three composed items: *The Canny Shepherd Laddie O The Hills*, which Willie believed was written by Mrs Nichols a shepherd's wife then of Cappercleuch who had given it to Willie in the early 60's, *Song of The Gillie More*, by the poet and scholar Hamish Henderson and *Herd Laddie O The Glen*, written by Willie himself just before he retired from Upper Monynut on the borders of East Lothian and Berwickshire. In this song Willie reflects on his working life and comments on the changes that have taken place in his lifetime.

REFLECTIONS ON SHEPHERDING

A left the school at Allanwater on the ninth of December 1910, that was before A wes twelve, an got a job switching trees for an ald man replanting a forest. Ma alder brither wes at hame taking odd jobs at the time but he went away onto water watching, aye a water bailiff to see that there was naebody poachin fish, an when he cam back there wes nothing do but what he would go to the police force, the chief constable wanted him. So the boss says tae ma faither "Well Jimmie," he says "juist keep the ither boy at hame, an let him bide," so - A had tae juist turn in as well. A had tae turn in and paddle ma own canoe.

A didna want tae be a shepherd at first. Well A'd been beatin at the holidays wi the shooters, drivin grouse, an A wes keen on shooting. We had a gun at home belonged tae me father an A wes gaun tae be a gamekeeper, that wes the only thing that A wanted tae do. A used tae go tae the rifle club at Skelfhill, it wes held in a long shed in the wintertime an outside in the summer an we whiles had a sing song efter. A mind singing *Owre the muir amang the heather* at one o the prize giving suppers - A'd be aboot thirteen - me aldest brother Tom used tae sing that song.

I wes always at home helping my father with herding as he wes very lame with rheumatic pains - unless I wes needed at the farm - an then A wud stay overnight there. They'd put me in aside the lad that worked the horses in the farmhoose. No matter what the men were daein A'd tae go an help; if it wes turning hay A'd tae learn tae turn hay; A'd got the wee pikes to build, the ricks o hay; or they'd be a man sittin makin hay ropes an ye'd got them tae twine - he keepit feedin in the hay an drawin back an feedin't - a rope as big as yer thumb o dry grass, an that wes tae tie the ricks doon. An then ye had yer own work to do as regards as

Shooting party: Willie, second from right.

getting in yer peats, yer fire in for the year; ye'd yer garden to look after, you grew all yer own potatoes; and if there wes a stone dyke fallen ye'd tae build it up again. If ther were bridges across the burn for the sheep, ye'd tae go and get timber in from the farm, cut it yersel, cart it oot an put the bridges back on again. The same if a fence or a post broke down, ye'd tae get them up again.

At that time me faither's wage wis thirty two pounds for the year. Jock me alder brither was a young shepherd an he had twenty two pounds for the year an A got for the year so much a week for cutting brecken, when the brecken wis on the job, an A got a wage for hill lambing. A'd got tae be at home for to assist me father if it wis stormy, an A cut sheep drains if it wis good days an him didnae need any assistance. A got 13/- for six hundred yards. If it come a bad winter, the ditches full aa the time, ye could dae nothing, but A wis helping him oot. I mind one winter for six months ma mother- she'd didna see anither woman aboot the place! She used to get half a ton o oatmeal an they got three hundredweight barrels o salt herrin and a barrel o paraffin in every year at October. Tatties an herrin wes yer staple diet. If ye bought herrin from the fishmonger in Hawick they were sixpence for a dozen, so ye mun ken how much cheaper they were getting three hundredweight in a barrel for thirty shillings, an that lasted ye the year if ye had nothing else tae eat.

A had no interest in the sheep whatever when A left the school you know but that ald farm manager that I was with - an me faither - well it wes the school of schools for me. The farm manager James McFarlane was a great stocks man and he gave you every encouragement to do everything juist right, which wes a great help to me for the rest of my life as a shepherd. He wes keen on showing sheep, mostly black faced ones and A got a great knowledge of dressing and preparing them for shows and sales.

He wes verra cute, he'd say "D'ye min me speakin aboot a guid sheep? bring it in, A'm gaun tae show it." Ye'd tae gae oot an puzzle yer brains. A always took the richt yin, but A sometimes took yin or twae extra. A got into his way an wherever a went ther wes no fermer foun fault wi me.

Kennin sheep… well its more or less a gift. There's some people giftit wi't, ye know, but it can be learnt. There's always something in th'expression of a sheep's face; its ears, or the way it walks an it's mebbe broader made as th'other ones. Aye it runs in families, they're great kenners. Names for sheep? well some sheep are more or less hereditary tae bad feet… A yuist tae caa them Jenny Mony feet; an a sorta yin that wasnae as it should thrive, ye know thinner es the rest, A caad them Dying Charlie… O ee'd various names for them; Jenny Geddes an different names. Ther waur a sheep, she jamp, ye couldnae keep her in nowhere. If ee gathert her tae do something the nixt day, she wes away in the morning, her an her lamb too. A caad her the Ald Jumper.

But, that ald fermer James McFarlane, wes verra strict, things had tae be dune the right way tae show it (sheep). We've mixed whiles half a dizzen stuffs up tae get the right colour, fur tae colour the sheep's coat. Ye dug aff the hillside- it wes naitural clay- juist the colour o the yoke o an egg. Well ee mix up the clay wi a liquid soap we bought, that an peat moss, tae the colour o a ripe field o wheat; it wisnae yellow ochre, it wes a wee bit darker as that. We pit it oan wi yon stirrup pump, juist like a fine mist, an when the coat's dry they'll shake thersels an it's lovely. Aa the time A wes sellin sheep everybody said tae me "Ye've made a grand job o weshin them sheep.

Sheep being driven to the Auction Mart through old Hawick

Whit dae ye colour them sheep wi?"

Well aboot 1916 I think it wes, I took the responsibility from ma faither that year for I wes often at the farm wi the sheep and he didn't come, but I had tae attend. It didnae matter whose sheep were going away, A'd tae go and give em a hand tae gether them up, get them to the farm to get sorted out for the market, and I'd tae drive them tae the market. A drove an awfie lot tae grass parks tae get them weaned off their mothers. Ye sortit one lot o lambs one day and they were markit – them that was tae go to the sales – and they were letit away to the hill, aa the small lambies, little wee dwarfie lambies were sent away aboot six miles yon side o Hawick tae grass parks wi'em. A cam back home, if A missed the sale well A'd tae walk the thirteen mile home. And A whiles wasna home when I'd tae get up and gaun away an give a hand tae gether another place, and the same the next place again.

Tup bred on Southalls farm, Strathaven, owned by James McFarlane, farmer of Hartwoodsmire when Willie worked there.

There used to be a three day sale at Hawick once a year in August, but there were ither sales too, every fortnight ye know. The three day big sale: cross lambs the first day, hill lambs the next day; and ewe lambs o aa breeds the next day. A wes away wi them the three days wi lambs at this grass park, then A'd tae get up an go an give the man that had the half breed lambs lower doon a hand tae gether his an put them along the shedder: where ye separate them from their mothers. Ye rin them them up a narrow place and there's a gate goes back an forth. Ye let the lambs in there an let the yowes go oan, an ye take the lambs away tae market.

Well as A wes saying ma faither wes bad wi arthritis and A got the chance of a job for a double herds' place at Allerybar, A took it and me faither did the boys place and A did the man's hirsel – among Cheviot sheep – but I didnae like them as well as the Blackies. A got seventy-five pound for the both of us, A had charge o counting the sheep. He had aboot twelve score o sheep that's aboot twae hundred and forty, an A had the rest aboot twenty-six score. A had tae assist him to do a portion o hill lambing, an A got a lambing man's wage for't, seiven pound for a month - me mother got twelve shilluns a week for keeping us - frae the farmer. A wes twae year there, and then A went away an got married an me faither went doon into Sunderland Hall tae look after two grass parks, he'd sheep comin in an he'd tae look after them, an me mother milked the cows for the mansion house.

Lambing started from aboot the first o April for the half bred yins and the hill lambing started on the eighteenth o April.

Sandy, ma younger brother hed left the school and started doing farm work and it was lambing time and the corbies wes eating the tongues oot o his lambs. He took me father's gun oot an he fell and the gun went off an the shot went straight through his leg. His dog cam back into the hoose barking an ma mither went up an she took his cords off wi yon hardy naperons, an she tied it tight roon his leg an got him back doon tae the hoose. She sent word doon tae the shepherd aboot half a mile doon the burn an he cam up and they carried him in the hoose, an somebody went for the doctor. He lay til the next day an the doctor said it couldna be saved, the poison o the powder had worked up the leg. He got his leg taken off at the hip in the hospital. It wis juist a wood leg he got tae begin wi, he made an stump an put a hoop on't for working an he worked for the County on the roads. A chap that was his chum - he wis a good fiddler - an anither fella wis a great accordion player an Sandy wis the drummer in this

Hawkhass, the Herd's house on Penchrise Farm; from here Willie left Allanwater School and started work in 1909 (the area is now under forestry)

wee band they had. But he always used tae come an lamb wi me, help me oot. We were aa shepherds.

Its quite common where the hoody craws will have the tongue off the lamb before its born - juist the head there – and the tongue oot – it'd be slippit off juist like it'd been cut off with a pair of scissors. They canna suck ye know, then they're as good as dead. Whenever the head appears if the tongues oot – corbies there - an its clippit off an away.

I had a bad back one year during the lambing an the farmer's son took the half of the hirsel. A had tae keep ma son Sandy off the school for to catch sheep for A couldna run or anything wi a bad back. An Sandy cam intae me cryin wi a big fine lamb in his arms, an A saw it wis kind of red at the bottom lip and A says "the corbies 'll've clippit it's tongue oot," an he was fair sad aboot that ye know. The corbies was in the wood, all high trees, an they came an they shot for two or three days. There were a lot o crows, ordinary crows, ye could gae into the bottom o the wood an see them makin away. They shot their guns off through the trees, an there was a lot of stoor come doon when they fired the shots up through the trees. O they took sackfuls away from that place.

Well ye see ye were employed for the twelve month, an whenever November came, the farmer made a new bargain wi ye for tae stay anither year; but that bargain didna start till the May term, that's like six months notice they were getting before yer next years contract, an six months tae look for a new man. An if ye werena stayin they'd mebbe be an advert, "Wanted for the twenty eighth o May" in one o the local papers. The back pages used tae be full o columns as to service at that time. A wis wi an employer - O A'd an awful job tae mak a bargain wi him right enough. I wis way him five years, an A'd tae gae doon tae the farm. He sent word up wi the post tae gae doon tae see him. An A wis mebbee three or fower times at the farm before A got a settlement. He was always sat on his hunkers wi a pencil figurin figures oot wi his thumb nail. When ye'd gotten a thing kinda settled up he'd've juist arisen an went an handed ye ten pound mebbe, it would've cost ye that tae flit tae another place. He wis really good that way, he'd gie ye ten pounds on the spot. This wis yer day at the hirin forbye.

Well when A wes with him he died an I wes left as his trustee tae look after the farm that year. A man took it an I wes wi him four year, but A wes boarding three o the children out for the school. It wes five mile to the school. A boarded them out during the winter and they walked during the summer from the Easter holidays to the summer holidays. They walked aboot five mile doon a wild burn - ten mile a day. They boarded wi a ploughman an his wife just across the road frae the school. The education allowed us half croon a week a piece an we paid seiven and six tae ten bob a week. At that time A had ninety four pound for the year.

After A left Braidliehope in 1927 they put a school bus on. It was a good place, up a burn certainly, house wasna fenced in nor nothing, cattle and bulls rinnin aboot the hills, but the salmon cam up by the very door. We didna want for fish from the October tae the New Year. Aboot February there wes great big yins come up… o fifty sixty pound weight.

Then there were a hiring day, you went tae it and the farmers would arrange tae meet ye there, an even if ye didnae want a place ye still went, it wis a day out. There were one at Hawick, what they'd caa

The school at Allanwater

the Herds day, and there were the Hinds day. There were a fair at Earlstoon the next week, a fair at Jedburgh an a fair at Coldstream. The Herds yin wis held after the New Year, the first Thurday in January, The Ploomans wis held the first Thursday in March. There wis a fair at Kelso, Annan and Dumfries - they were aa places ye could gaun tae - ye got the day off if ye were needin a place. Ye'd gae first thing in the morning an it wis last thing at night before it stoppit. The farmer took ye intae the hotel an made a bargain wi ye. It wis a case ye mebbe had therty bob a week an ye wanted therty-five, well ye opened yer mooth wide enough tae begin wi, an ye could come doon a wee bit, an ye whiles had tae half the difference. Ye couldna make a yin withoot halfin the difference in the finish. A lot o them gied ye a pound juist because it was yer expenses at the hirin fair. At Copshie Fair at one time they had tae have a straw in their mouth them that wis wantin a maid's job. A woman would stand in the square yonder wi a straw in her mouth. Ma mither went to Copshie Fair for hirin.

The first time A can remember gaun tae Copshie (Copshawholm) wes aboot nineteen five. A went there wi me faither til a sheep sale. He drove the sheep owre the hill t'Newcastleton frae Lodgegill. Well later on A wes tae live there twinty seiven – twinty six year in the valley; an there's no place like Cophshieholm. A talk aboot gan back hame- gan there.

At one time it was all walking. When I worked at the Holm (Copshieholm) A was the only herd looking after 4,000 acres and had 700 black-faced sheep .

Aye we could have bad winters. Ane winter - we were at Windshielknowe an it was a particularly bad winter - well ane night there were 173 sheep buried in the snow and A found them all by noon the next day. Sheep dogs saved me in all sorts of ways when A was a herd. A had one which could mark sheep stuck in the snow. A trained aa my own dogs – they hae t'hae a kinna naitural wycenis forbye the trainin. They're fer easier traint if they're kinna naitural wyce and hardy tae. They have tae be hardy - well the kinna way that they've sub bred them fur sheep dog trials, they're that soft that ee'd hae t'hae aboot half a dizzen if ee wantit tae git a days work dune. They bred them fur tae mak them easy control. Til they're es sib as mice!

These reminiscences are just a small selection from my taped interviews with Willie. He had a remarkable memory, pinpointing details that gave an accurate account of a way of life now gone. He was not given to exaggeration and his droll manner and dry humour served to highlight the integrity and pride he felt in his life's work.

Willie told me that "the sheep were ma life, ma work; the songs were a by product - a song's no worth nothing to anybody unless its expressed - it's the feeling and the expression that makes the song." His song collection portrays a long tradition that has expressed people's hardships and love stories; their humour and sadness; their sense of history and connection with the land.

It has been a great privilege on my part to have been Willie's scribe; to bear witness (when he was an old man) to his remarkable ability to continually learn new songs and take up new situations. He was a unique figure whose significant presence at the time of the Folksong Revival bridged the old world with the new - a masterly tradition bearer of the songs and lore of the Borders. Willie Scott was both a friend and a mentor, and as I write I am reminded of listening to him recite in his 91st year *The Drouthie Driver* yet another unexpected piece from the recesses of his memory. He was indeed a "gey ald warrior". This revised edition pays tribute to the memory of ...

Willie Scott, Liddesdale Shepherd and Singer.

THE SONGS

Singing at Whitby
Festival in 1978

Sweet Copshawholm

Sae brightly shines the simmer's sun
Oot owre the hill an plain,
An sweetly frae the lift abuin
Is heard the laiverock's strain.
Aa night A wander forth mysel
Where lowin cattle roam,
An view the spot I lo'e so well,
My native Copshawholm.

It nestles in amang the hills
Where Liddel stream doth glide,
Through grassy mead and rocky dell
To join the Solway tide.
An aa aroon, baith near an far
Neath Heaven's lofty dome,
There is a spell sae peacefu here
I love thee, Copshawholm.

I've wandered east, I've wandered west
An mony places seen
Aa in their summer grandeur dressed
Wi flooers an bushies green;
By mairlan wide an mountain steep,
Where ocean's billow roams
Abuin them aa I prize a peep
O thee, sweet Copshawholm.

Each neebor kens his neebor's lot
An coonts him as a freen;
'Tis pleasant tae sey each cot
Sae tidy, neat and clean.
What though a lowly life they lead
In a village of the loam?
There's compensation sweet indeed
In thee, sweet Copshawholm.

Tae mey it is a sweet content
Acquaintance tae renew,
Where youth's sunny days were spent
Mang people kind and true;
But there is not work for all
And youth must wander from
Their place of birth, at duty's call,
And leave the Copshawholm.

Fareweel thou spot I lo'e so dear
For I maun haste away,
When city strife falls on the ear
I have my part to play;
And as I find my years increase
I'll dream of times to come,
When I shall end my days in peace
In thee, sweet Copshawholm.

The Soft Lowland Tongue O The Borders

How often a wanderer comes back and dreams tae the banks whaur the hazels are growin
Whaur Teviot, Gala, or Jed's bonny streams whaur Tweed's crystal waters are row - in.
We hear the auld tongue frae the stoot Border lad as he follows the plough or the har - row,
The Border lass sings it in strains sweet or sad on the banks o the Ett - rick or Yar - row.

chorus:
What_ though in the ha's o the great we may meet wi men o high rank and braw or - ders
Oor hearts aye for hame and nae mu - sic sae sweet, As the soft low - land tongue o the Bor - ders.

FORM: verse 1 - A B A A' chorus ; verse 2 - A A' B B' chorus ; verse 3 - A B' A B' chorus

How often a wanderer comes back and dreams
Tae the banks whaur the hazels are growin;
Whaur Teviot, Gala, or Jed's bonnie streams
Whaur Tweed's crystal waters are rowin.
We hear the auld tongue frae the stoot Border lad
As he follows the plough or the harrow;
The Border lass sings it in strains sweet or sad,
On the banks o the Ettrick or Yarrow.

Chorus

What though in the ha's o the great we may meet
Wi men o high rank and braw orders;
Oor herts aye for hame and nae music sae sweet,
As the soft lowland tongue o the Borders.

O blithe is the lilt o his ain mother tongue
To the exile that's lang been a roaming;
It brings aye to mind, the hall sangs that were sung
From his faither's fireside in the gloamin.
It brings back the scent o the heathery breeze;
The sound o the wee burnie's whimple;
The lauchan and dauchan o youth's happy days,
When his cheek's deepest line wis a dimple.

Chorus

It's the tongue that was spoken by Leyden and Scott;
By Hogg near the lonely St Marys,
Shall ne'er by true Border hearts be forgot
Though there's times where the changes may vary.
And lang may sweet peace and prosperity reign,
And keep aa oor hames frae disorder,
And lang may we welcome that auld wordly strain:
The soft lowland tongue o the Borders.

Chorus

Copshawholm Fair

On a Friday it fell in the month of April,

Owre the hills cam the morn wi her blithesomest smile;

The folks were aa thranging the roads everywhere

Makin haste tae be in at the Copshawholm Fair.

They were seen comin in frae the mountains and glens,

Baith rosie faced lassies and strappin young men;

Aa jumpin wi joy and unburdened wi care,

When meeting auld freens at the Copshawholm Fair.

Tis a day when auld courtships are often renewed,
Disputes set aside or more hotly pursued;
What Barleycorn Johnny sees fit tae declare
Is law for he's king at the Copshawholm Fair.
There are lads for the lassies and toys for the bairns;
There's blin ballad singers and folk wi no airms,
A fiddler is here, an a thimbler is there,
Wi nutmen an spicemen at Copshawholm Fair.

There's pethers an potters an gingerbreid stans,
Peepshows, puff an darts an great caravans;
There's fruit frae aa nations exhibited there
And kail plants frae Hawick at the Copshawholm Fair.
Noo aboot the hirin if you want tae hear tell
Ye shall ken it as fer as A've seen it masel;
That whit wages are gien, it is ill tae declare,
Sae muckle they vary at Copshawholm Fair.

Only yin A saw hirin a strappin young quine,
Heard her speir whit her age wis an whaur she had been;
Whit work she'd been daein an how lang she'd been there,
Whit wages she wanted at Copshawholm Fair.
At first the young lassie a wee while stood dumb.
She blushed an she scrappit her fit on the grun;
At last she took hairt an did stoutly declare
"A'll hae five pund an ten at Copshawholm Fair."

Says he, "But my lass that's a verra big wage,"
And turnin about as he'd been in a rage,
Says, "A'll gie ye five pund, but A'll gie ye nae mair
A think ye maun tak it this Copshawholm Fair."
He held out the shillun tae arle the bit wench
In case it should enter her noddle tae flinch;
She grap at it mutterin "I shoulda haen mair
But yet A will tak it at Copshawholm Fair."

Noo the hirin wis dune and aff they aa sprang,
They run tae the bar room tae jine in the thrang;
"I never will lie wi my mammy nae mair,"
The fiddler plays briskly at Copshawholm Fair.
There's one in the corner sits drinkin his gill,
Anither beside him sits sippin his yill;
Anither is strippit an swearin richt sair
"Room will ye no gie me at the Copshawholm Fair."

Noo this is the fashion they thus passed the day
Till nicht comes at last and they ellie away;
But some are sae sick that they canna dae mair
Wi dancin an fechtin at Copshawholm Fair.

Castleton Hiring Fair, known as Copshawholm Fair, photographed around 1902 by Dr Rufus Evans. It was held either the second Friday in April or the Friday before the 17th of May.
The last 'Copshie' Fair took place in 1912.

When The Kye Cams Hame

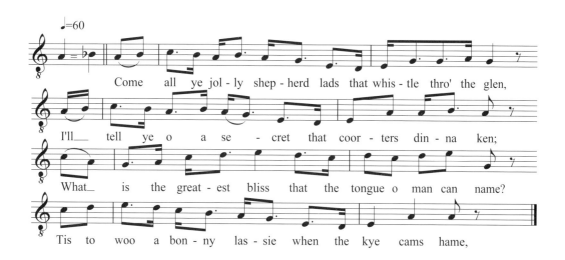

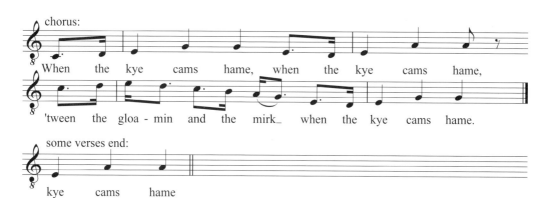

Come all ye jolly shepherd lads that whistles thro' the glen,

I'll tell you o a secret that coorters dinna ken;

What is the greatest bliss that the tongue of man can name?

Tis to woo a bonnie lassie when the kye cams hame.

Chorus

When the kye cams hame, when the kye cams hame,

Tween the gloaming and the mirk, when the kye cams hame.

Tis not beneath the burgonet nor yet beneath the crown,
Tis not on couch of velvet nor yet on bed of down:
Tis beneath the spreading birch in the dell withoot a name,
Wi a bonnie, bonnie lassie, when the kye cams hame.

Chorus

Then the eyes shine sae bright the hail soul to beguile,
There's love in every whisper and joy in every smile;
O who could choose a crown wi its perils and its fame,
And miss a bonnie lassie, when the kye cams hame.

Chorus

See ye yonder pawky shepherd that lingers on the hill,
His yowes are in the fauld and his lambs are lying still;
Yet he daurna gang tae rest for his heart is in a flame
To meet his bonnie lassie when the kye cams hame.

Chorus

Ah, awa with fame and fortune, what comfort can they gie?
And aa the arts that prey on man's life and liberty?
Gie me the highest joy that the heart of man can frame,
My bonnie, bonnie lassie, when the kye cams hame.

Chorus

Twas On Yin Night In Sweet July

the Brundenlaws

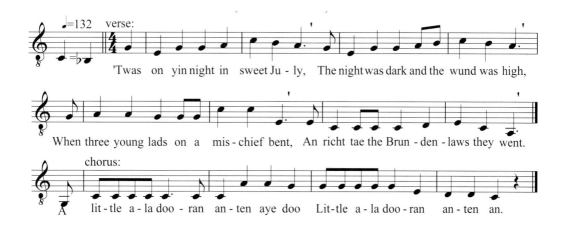

Twas on yin night in sweet July,

The night was dark and the wund was high,

When three young lads on a mischief bent

An richt tae the Brundenlaws they went.

> *Chorus*
>
> A little ala dooran anten aye doo
>
> Little ala dooran anten an.

Straught for a ladder they did go,

An placed agin the window sole;

Then Pete tae the top o the ladder did rin

Sayin 'Hey bonnie lassies will ye no let us in ?'

> *Chorus*

We chaffed them up till efter two,

Till daylight it was breaking through;

Then Pete says 'Fareweel, we're awa for shair '

When they heard auld Tam coming up the stair.

> *Chorus*

Doon the ladder fast we ran,
Say 'Run boys run for here comes Tam;'
So awa like hares we did gang,
And hid in the field whaur the hay was lang.

Chorus

We crept thegither tae form a plan,
Tae see wha back for the ladder wid gang;
Says I 'A'll tell ye whit we'll dae –
We'll fling the damn auld ladder away !'

Chorus

Nae suiner was this plan proposed
Till yin tae each end o the ladder goes;
And carried it right oot o sight,
And threw the damned thing owre the dyke.

Chorus

Next morn when auld Tam arose,
Straight tae the broken ladder he goes;
And when he saw it lying there,
He cursed and he swore and he tore his hair.

Chorus

Then straight tae the cook wi aa his might,
Sayin 'Jean last night's been an awfu night;
Sae sit ye doon and tell me plain,
An gie tae me every yin o their names.'

Chorus

'Tae gie their names A'll dae whit A can,
But A'll no tell owre mony, for fear A'm wrang;
There was Geid frae the Hass and Pete frae the Hill;
And young Wullie Scott frae the auld sawmill.'

Chorus

Then aff tae Willie Wilson he did steer,
Sayin 'Hey man gang and saddle the mere,
For I maun ride tae Jeddart an gie them in,
For the breakin o the ladder at the Brundenlaws.'

Chorus

Next day a policeman tae me did come,
Says 'Pete ma man whit have ye done?
Just come tae Jethart and plead yer cause,
For breaking the ladder at the Brundenlaws.'

Chorus

'For breaking the ladder man, whit's this ye say?
A never heard tell o't till this very day,
So if ye think that I'm the man,
Baith you and Tam Charlton's damn far wrang!'

Chorus

Noo here's tae the lads and lassies dear
A've nae mair news for ye tae hear;
But if ye gang oot skealin waas,
Keep awa frae Tam Charlton o the Brundenlaws.

Chorus

The Dowie Dens O Yarrow

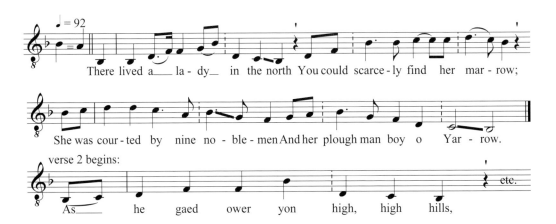

There lived a la-dy in the north You could scarce-ly find her mar-row;
She was cour-ted by nine no-ble-men And her plough man boy o Yar-row.

verse 2 begins:
As he gaed ower yon high, high hills,

There lived a lady in the north
You could scarcely find her marrow;
She was courted by nine noblemen
And her ploughman boy o Yarrow.

As he gaed owre yon high, high hills,
An doon yon path sae narrow;
There he spied nine noblemen
For to fight with him on Yarrow.

There was three he slew, and three withdrew,
And three lay dyin wounded;
Till her brother John stepped in behind
An pierced his body through.

"Go home, go home, you false young man,
An tell your sister sorrow:
That her true love John lies dead and gone
And a bloody corpse on Yarrow."

As he gaed owre yon high, high hills,
And doon yon path sae narrow;
There he spied his sister dear
She was comin fast for Yarrow.

"O brother dear I've dreamt a dream
An I hope it won't prove sorrow:
I dreamt that you were spilling bluid
On the dowie dens of Yarrow."

"O sister dear I'll read your dream
And I'm sure it will prove sorrow:
Your true love John lies dead and gone
And a bloody corpse on Yarrow."

Now this fair maid's hair was three quarters long
And the colour of it was yellow;
She tied it roon his middle smaa
An she cairried him hame tae Yarrow.

"O daughter dear dry up your tears
An dwell no more in sorrow;
For I'll wed you tae a far higher degree
Than your ploughman boy on Yarrow."

"O faither dear you have seven sons
You can wed them all tomorrow,
But a fairer flooer there never bloomed
Than my ploughman boy on Yarrow."

When Fortune Turns Her Wheel

Come fill a glass let's drink about
This night we'll merry be,
For harmony and freenship free
Likewise my comrades three;
To meet ye aa aince mair ma freens
A sacred joy I feel,
Tho far awa I noo maun stray
Till Forturne turns her wheel.

The changes of a comrade state
Ne'er mak true freenship less,
For a true Caledonian's heart
Feels warmer for distress;
For I hae met some trusty freens
And tae me they've aye been leal,
Though far awa I noo maun stray
Till Fortune turns her wheel.

Tis not vain clothes nor gold he says
That's the estimate o man;
For when we meet a freen in straits
We shake a freenly hand;
Wi them I'll sit, wi them we drink
And tae them our minds reveal,
And freens we'll be whatever way
Blind Fortune turns her wheel.

But, o I loved a bonnie lass
And her I'll justly blame;
For when hard fortune on me frowned
She denied she kent my name;
But falsehood by remorse is paid
And tae her I'll never kneel,
I'll sweethearts find, baith fair and kind,
When Fortune turns her wheel.

It's mony the time my heart's been sair
And like tae brak in twa;
Mony's the time my feet's been cauld
Comin in frae the frost and snaw;
Wi nae yin tae pity me
Not yet to wish me weel,
But maybe I'll repay them back
When Fortune turns the wheel.

Some of my pretended freens
If freens I may them caa,
Proved false and turned their backs on me
When mine was at the waa;
But in a glass I'll let it pass
I'm sure I wish them weel,
If my hard fate on them await
May Fortune turn her wheel.

Adieu, ye hills o Caledonia
Likewise sweet Avondale,
For freenship binds the strongest ties
Love tells the softest tale;
Adieu, my freens and comrades here,
I ken ye wish me weel
And maybe yet, can pay my debt
When Fortune turns her wheel.

Pulling Hard Against The Stream

In this world I've gained my know-ledge and for it___ I've had to pay:

Though I ne-ver went to col-lege I have heard_ the po-et say,

Life is like a migh-ty ri-ver rol-ling on from day to day,

Men are ves-sels launched u-pon it Some-times wrecked and cast a-way.

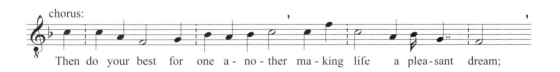

Then do your best for one a-no-ther ma-king life a plea-sant dream;

Help a worn and wea-ry bro-ther pul-ling hard_ a-gainst the stream.

Mo-ny a bright good hair-ted fel-low...

In this world I've gained my knowledge
And for it I've had to pay;
Though I never went to college
I have heard the poet say,
Life is like a mighty river
Rolling on from day to day,
Men are vessels launched upon it
Sometimes wreck'd and cast away.

Chorus
    Then do your best for one another
    Making life a pleasant dream;
    Help a worn and weary brother
    Pulling hard against the stream.

Mony a bright guid hairted fellow,
Mony a noble minded man,
Finds himself in waters shallow
Then assist him if you can;
Some succeed at every turning
Fortune favours every scheme,
Not a friend and not a shilling
Pulling hard against the stream.

Chorus

If the wind is in your favour
And you've weather'd every squall,
Think of those who luckless labour
Never get fair wind at all;
Working hard contented willing,
Struggling through life's ocean wide,
Not a friend and not a shilling
Pulling hard against the tide.

Chorus

Don't give way to foolish sorrow
Let this keep you in good cheer;
Brighter days may come tomorrow
If you try and persevere.
Darkest nights must have a morning
Though the sky be overcast;
Lowest days must have a turning,
And the tide will turn at last.

Chorus

Jimmie Raeburn

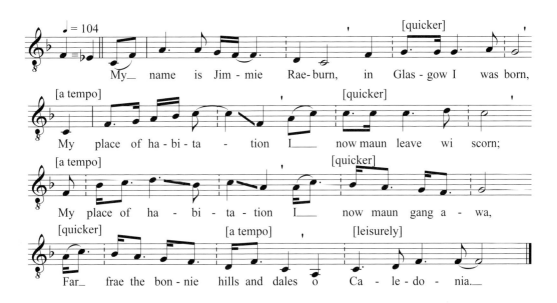

My_ name is Jim - mie Rae - burn, in Glas - gow I was born,
My place of ha - bi - ta - tion I_ now maun leave wi scorn;
My place of ha - bi - ta - tion I_ now maun gang a - wa,
Far_ frae the bon - nie hills and dales o Ca - le - do - nia._

verse 2 and all subsequent verses begin:

It was...

My name is Jimmie Raeburn, in Glasgow I was born,

My place of habitation I now maun leave wi scorn,

My place of habitation I now maun gang awa,

Far frae the bonnie hills and dales o Caledonia.

It was early one morning, just by the break o day,

I overheard the turnkey who unto us did say,

"Arise ye helpless convicts, arise ye yin an aa

This is the day that we maun stray frae Caledonia."

We all arose pit on oor clothes, oor herts were filled wi grief,

An aa oor freens stood roon the coach, tae grant us nae relief,

An aa oor freens stood roon the coach, tae see us gang away,

Tae see us leave the hills and dales o Caledonia.

Farewell, my aged mother, I'm vexed for what I've done.
I hope none will upcast on you, the race that I have run;
I hope God will protect you, when I am far awa,
Far frae the bonnie hills and dales o Caledonia.

Fareweel my aged faither, he is the best o men,
And likewise my sweetheart, young Catherine is her name;
Nae mair I'll walk by Clyde's clear streams, or by the Broomielaw,
Fareweel my freens, ye hills and dales o Caledonia.

But o perchance we'll meet again, I hope twill be above,
Where hallelujahs will be sung tae Him wha reigns in love;
Nae earthly judge shall judge us there, but Him wha rules us all,
Fareweel my freens, ye hills and dales of Caledonia.

Jim and Ellen Scott with five of their seven children:
(from left to right) cousin Nell, Jock, Sandy, Mat ,Willie and Cis. Taken at Hawkhass about 1913.

Time Wears Awa

Oh but the oors rin fast awa
Like the Kelvin tae the Clyde,
Sin on its bonnie gowan banks
I wooed thee for my bride;
My ain dear love sae sweet and young
Sae artless and sae fair,
Then love was aa the grief we kent
And you my only care.

Chorus
Time wears awa, time wears awa,
An winna let us be,
It stole the wild rose frae my cheek
And the blithe blink frae your ee.

When woods were green and flooers fair
While you were aa my ain;
I little reckoned what years would bring
O poortith toil and pain.
Some waefu oors hae flapped their wings
Dark shadows owre oor lot,
Sin like twa cushats o the glen
We strayed in this dear spot.

Chorus

The voices o these happy days
Steal on oor dreams by night;
And cherished mem'ries rise and glow
Wi their depairted light.
But still the birds and burnies sing
Their wildered melodies,
As in the gowden dawn o life
When we were young and free.

Chorus

Hawkhass, the Herd's house on Penchrise Farm; from here Willie left Alanwater
School and started work in 1909. (the area is now under forestry)

Come Aa Ye Tramps And Hawkers

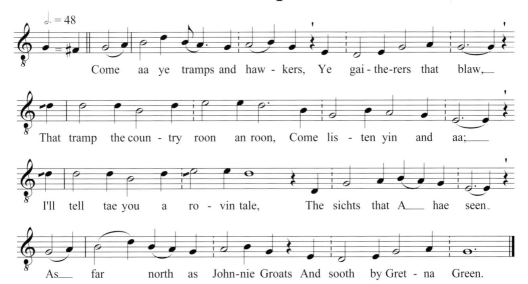

Come aa ye tramps and haw-kers, Ye gai-the-rers that blaw,
That tramp the coun-try roon an roon, Come lis-ten yin and aa;
I'll tell tae you a ro-vin tale, The sichts that A hae seen,
As far north as John-nie Groats And sooth by Gret-na Green.

Come aa ye tramps and hawkers
Ye gaitherers that blaw,
That tramp the country roon an roon,
Come listen yin and aa;
I'll tell tae you a rovin tale,
The sichts that A hae seen,
As far north as Johnnie Groats
And sooth by Gretna Green.

I hae passed the bold Ben Nevis
Wi his shouther tae the moon;
I've tramped by Crieff and Callander
An roon by bonnie Doon;
I've chanted roon by Ettrick Shaws
An up by Tushie Law,
But the bonniest lassie e'er I saw
Was in bonnie Gallowa.

Aftimes I've laughed untae masel
When trudgin on the road;
My toe-rags roon my blistered feet,
My face as broon's a toad;

Wi lumps o cake and tattie scones
And whangs o braxy ham,
Nae thocht o whaur I'd come frae
Or kent I whaur I was gaun.

I've done my share o humphin
Wi the dockers on the Clyde;
I helpit Buckie trawlers
Pu their herrin owre the side;
I helped tae build the michty brig
That spans the busy Forth,
And wi mony eident fairmer trig
I've plooed at Elmford.

It's lovely in the summer time
Aneath the bright blue sky;
No kennin in the mornin
Where at nicht ye hae tae lie;
In byre or barn or onywhere,
Dossin in amang the hay,
But if the weather plays me fair
I'm happy aa the day.

51

Tinker's Waddin

In June when broom in bloom was seen and bracken was fu' fresh and green,
And warm the sun with silver sheen the hills and glens did gladden o;
Yin day upon the Border bent the tinkers pitched their gypsy tent,
And old and young with ae consent resolved tae hae a waddin o.

Chorus
> Der ma doo, ma doo, ma day, der ma doo ma daddy o,
> Der ma doo, ma doo, ma day, hoorah for the tinker's waddin o.

The bridegroom was wild Norman Scott, wha thrice had broke the nuptial knot,
And yince was sentenced tae be shot, for breach o martial order o.
His gleesom jo she was Madge McKell, a speywife match for Nick himsel,
Wi glamour and cantrip, charm and spell, she frichted baith the Border o.

Chorus

Nae priest was there with solemn face nae clerk to claim o crouns the brace,
The piper and fiddler played the grace to set their gabs asteerin o.
'Mang beef and mutton, pork and veal, 'mang paunches, plucks and fresh cowheel,
Fat haggis and a cauler jeel, they carried awa careerin o.

Chorus

Fresh salmon newly taen in Tweed saut ling and cod o Shetland breed,
They worried till kites were like tae screed 'mang flagons and flasks o gravy o.
There was raisin kail and sweet milk saps, and yowe milk cheese in whangs and flaps,
And they rubbit their guts 'mang gabs and scraps, richt mony a cadger's cavey o.

Chorus

The drink flew roond in wild galore and soon upraised a hideous roar,
Blithe Comus saw ne'er a queerer core, seated roond his table o.
They drank, they danced, they swore, they sang, they quarreled and 'greed the whole day lang,
And they wrangled and tangled amang the thrang, wad match the tongues o Babel o.

Chorus

Noo the drink went doon before their drouth and vexed baith mony a maw and mooth,
It dampit the fire o age and youth and every breist did sadden o.
Till three stout loons flew o'er the fell, at risk o life their drouth tae quell,
And robbin a neebourin smuggler's still tae cairry on the waddin-o.

Chorus

Wi thunderous shouts they hailed them back, tae broach the barrels they werena slack,
While the fiddler's plane-tree leg they brak for playing 'Fareweel Tae Whisky O'
Delerium seized the uproarious thrang, the bagpipes in the fire they flang,
And they wrangled and tangled amang the thrang, the drink played siccan a pliskey o.

Chorus

Noo the sun fell laich o'er Solway's banks, while on they plyed their roughsome pranks,
And the stalwart shadows o their shanks wide o'er the muir was spreadin o.
Till heids and thraws amang the whins, they fell wi broken brows and shins,
And sair cast banes filled mony skins, at the close o the Tinker's waddin o.

Chorus

Lock The Door Lariston

Lock the door, Lar- is- ton, li on of Lid- desdale, Lock the door Lar -is- ton, Low- ther comes on;

The Arm- strongs are fly- ing their wi- dows are cry ing, The Cas- tle- ton's bur- ning and O - li ver's gone.

Lock the door, Lar- is- ton, high on the wea- ther gleam, See how the Sax -on plumes bob in the sky.

Yeo - man and car - bi- neer, Bill- man and   Hal- bar- dier   Fierce is the fo- ray and far is the cry.

line 3 of verses 2 and 4 begins:

Lock the door, Lariston, lion of Liddesdale,

Lock the door Lariston, Lowther comes on;

The Armstrongs are flying, their widows are crying,

The Castleton's burning and Oliver's gone.

Lock the door, Lariston, high on the weather gleam

See how the Saxon plumes bob in the sky;

Yeoman and carbineer, Billman and Halbardier

Fierce is the foray and far is the cry.

Bewcastle brandishes high his broad scimitar,

Ridley is riding his fleet footed grey;

Hedley and Howard there, Wandle and Windermere,

Lock the door, Lariston, hold them at bay;

Why dost thou smile, noble Elliot of Lariston

Why do the joy-candles gleam in thine eye?

Thou bold Border ranger, beware o thy danger,

Thy foes are relentless, determined and nigh.

I've Mangerton, Gorrenberry, Raeburn and Netherby,
Old Sim of Whittram, and all his array;
Come all Northumberland, Teesdale and Cumberland
Here at the Breaken Tower end shall the fray.
Scowled the broad sun o'er the links of green Liddesdale
Red as the beacon-light tipp'd he the wold;
Many a bold martial eye, mirror'd that morning sky
Never more oped on his orbit of gold.

Shrill was the bugle's note, dreadful the warrior shout,
Lances and halberds in splinters were borne;
Halberd and hauberk then, braved the claymore in vain
Buckler and armlet in shivers were shorn;
See how they wane, in the proud files of the Windermere
Howard – Ah woe to thy hopes of the day.
Hear the wide welkin rend, while the Scots' shouts ascend
"Elliot o Lariston, Elliot for aye."

Hermitage Castle

air: Come Aa Ye Tramps and Hawkers

Aa four square walls of Hermitage
Stand stout and steep today;
Wherein within the sheltered walls
The wounded Bothwell lay.
The whaups will cry sae mournfully
The river runs as broon;
As when the willing slave of love
A queen cam riding doon.

To Hermitage, to Hermitage
The river laughed in glee;
The beaches tossed their crimson flags
And glad at heart was she;
The hooves made music down the glen
Their bits were jingling gay;
From Jedburgh to Hermitage
That bright October day.

To Hermitage to Hermitage
What fears of robbers bold;
With buckler sword and Huntley's spear
The right of way to hold.
What raider on the Border moss
Would so and gallant prove;
As crossed a shaft of beauty
On the road that leads to love.

Now wave white hand to Hermitage
The watcher on the tower,
Shall wake the wounded warden
At the rapture of the hour;
What het can burn sae bitterly?
What steel can stab sae deep?
But love must bear the sting o it
The watcher on the keep.

Wide wound the road to Hermitage
The jingling bits are done;
A ghostly band may cross the hill
And none will see them come;
And none will see that white hand wave
Or from the rampart turn
With tidings o the phantom troops
That ride the Braidley burn.

Part of the stone circle 'Nine Stane Rig' (now surrounded by forestry).
"A wes herdin at the hirsel whaur Lord Sowlis wes boilt,
Nine Stane Rig at Hermitage.

An they rowed 'im in a sheet o leid fur a funeral pall
They plunged 'im in the caaldron red
An meltit 'im leid an bones an all

That wes juist oot frae the hoose whaur A lived, an the pot he was boilt in's stannin
at Skelfhill for watering cattle."

During the 13th century the Lordship of Liddesdale belonged to the family of De Soulis. Hermitage Castle has always been associated with the warlock, Lord Soulis. One of his crimes was to invite 'The Cout of Keilder' to a feast, then murder him in the nearby pool by holding him under the water with spears until dead. "The Cowt o Keilder wes buirit ootside the chapel: hey wes that big, ten fuit lang, they couldnae bury 'im inside the chapel." Legend has it that Lord Soulis was executed by boiling him alive as described by Willie. The pool, grave and chapel lie just off the top right hand corner of the photograph. Land lying to the left of the Castle is known in the Scott family as "The Spiritland".

There's Bound To Be A Row

I'm a poor un-luc-ky mar-ried man I've such an aw-ful wife,
To please her I do all I can And still she plagues my life;
If I do eve-ry-thing that's right She'll find a fault some-how,
And if I just stay out all night There's bound to be a row.

chorus:
There's bound to be a row, There's bound to be a row,
Do all in my life for to please my wife And there's bound to be a row.

I'm a poor unlucky man
I've such an awful wife;
To please her I do all I can
And still she plagues my life.
If I do everything that's right
She'll find a fault somehow;
And if I just stay out all night
There's bound to be a row.

She wakes me in the morning
In an awful cruel way;
She kicks me on the floor
And not a hard word do I say.
I have to wash my stockings,
My shirts and fronts I vow;
And if I don't wash hers as well
There's bound to be a row.

Chorus

There's bound to be a row,
There's bound to be a row,
Do all in my life for to please my wife
And there's bound to be a row.

Chorus

She has taken in a lodger
And he's single by the by;
She says I must make room for him
And on the sofa lie.
They eat the meat give me the bones,
It don't seem right somehow;
And if I just say half as much
There's bound to be a row.

    Chorus

She sometimes makes a party
To some friends that dine at eight;
And I've to hurry home from work
For to be in time to wait.
And as they hustle me about
If I don't scrape and bow
And say 'Yes sir' and 'Thank you please'
There's bound to be a row.

    Chorus

Then after I've earned my wages;
After working hard all week,
I turn in every hap-ny up
And then she has the cheek:
To give me tuppence to myself
And for that I've got to bow,
And if I spend it all at yince
There's bound to be a row.

    Chorus

Johnny Raw

A'm Johnny Raw a ceevil chiel, I was brocht up in the country,
Nae doot ye wadna ken me weel, for A'm aa the way frae Fintry;
Although A'm bowsie, yet A'm fly, among the lassies A do pry
And efter me they aa do cry, "I wish yer Granny saw ye!"

Chorus

Tuts gae awa! d'ye mean tae blaw?
A ken ye're up tae a thing or twa;
As shair as daith noo, Johnny Raw
I wish yer Granny saw ye!

A lo'ed a lass a gey lang time, she was a cairter's dochter,
At last A thocht A'd mak her mine, and a wooden ring A bocht her;
Says I, "My lass, now be sincere, just name the day and I'll be your dear,"
But she laughed and whispered in my ear, "I wish yer Granny saw ye!"

Chorus

Ae nicht as A walked doon Argyle Street, a lady said "Do please sir –
O would you hold my little baby sweet? for I'm feart the crood might squeeze her."
A took the bairn and said I would, A like tae dae aa the lassies guid,
And as we went pushing through the crood, she says, "I wish yer Granny saw ye!"

Chorus

As we went pushing through the crood, somehow A missed the lady,
Quite wonderstruck and there A stood, she'd left me with the baby!
The crood all gethered roond aboot, and laughed at my condition
Till up cam two policeman stoot and took me tae the station.
Tae laugh at me they all began, they said I was a lucky man
Tae get a wean brocht tae me han, "I wish yer Granny saw ye!"

Chorus

Before the bailiffs the next day A made my simple statement
Of how the lady ran away, and left me with the infant;
And then the Bailiff he did say, "You and the child may go away,
Find a nurse and for her pay, "I wish yer Granny saw ye!"

Chorus

Donald's Return To Glencoe

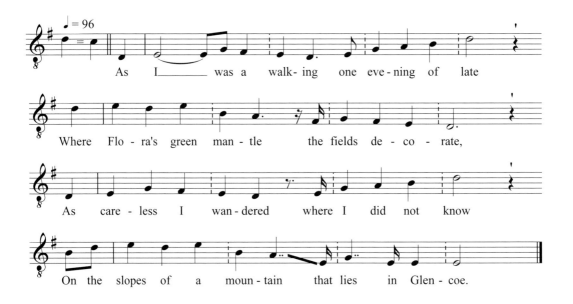

As I was a-walking one evening of late,
Where Flora's green mantle the fields decorate;
As careless I wandered where I did not know,
On the slopes of a mountain that lies in Glencoe.

Like her who the prize of Mount Ida had won,
There approached me a lassie as bright as the sun;
The ribbons and tartans around her did flow,
It won the heart of the pride of Glencoe.

With courage undaunted to her I drew nigh,
The red rose and lily on her cheek seemed to vie;
If your young affection on me you'll bestow
You'll aye bless the hour that we met in Glencoe.

"Young man," she made answer, "Your suit I disdain,
I once had a true love young Donald by name.
He sailed to the wars about ten years ago,
And a maid I remain till he returns to Glencoe."

"Perhaps your young Donald regards not your name
And has placed his affections on some foreign dame;
And may hae forgotten, for ought that ye know,
The lovely young lassie that he left in Glencoe."

"My Donald can never from his promise depart,
For love, truth and honour was found in his heart;
And if I ne'er see him I single will go,
And mourn for my Donald, the pride of Glencoe."

"Oh but the French they are hard to pull down,
They caused many brave heroes to die from their wounds;
And with your young Donald it may have been so
That on some foreign field, perhaps he's laid low."

So finding her constant, he pulled out a glove
Which in parting she gave him as a token of love;
She fell on his breast and the tears down did flow
Saying, "You are my Donald returned to Glencoe."

"Come cheer up dear Flora, your sorrows are o'er
While life shall remain we will never part more;
The loud sounds of war at a distance may roar,
But we'll ne'er leave the mountains that lie in Glencoe."

The Band O Shearers

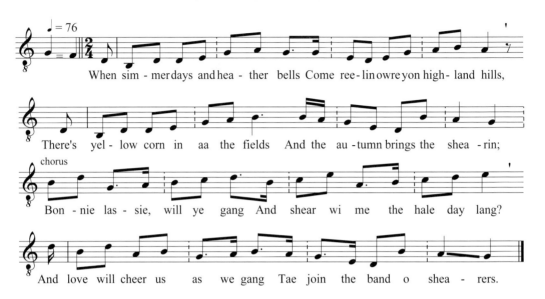

When sim - mer days and hea - ther bells Come ree - lin owre yon high- land hills,

There's yel - low corn in aa the fields And the au -tumn brings the shea - rin;

chorus
Bon - nie las - sie, will ye gang And shear wi me the hale day lang?

And love will cheer us as we gang Tae join the band o shea - rers.

When simmer days and heather bells
Come reelin owre yon highland hills;
There's yellow corn in aa the fields
And the autumn brings the shearin;

Chorus
　Bonnie lassie, will ye gang
　And shear wi me the hale day lang?
　And love will cheer us as we gang
　Tae join the band o shearers.

And gin the weather it be hot
I'll cast ma gravat and cast ma coat;
And we will join the happy lot
As they gang tae the shearin.

Chorus

And gin the thistle be owre strang
An pierce your lily, milkwhite hand;
It's wi my hook I'll cut it doon
As we gang tae the band of shearers.

Chorus

An if the folk wha's passin by
Say there is love 'tween ye and I;
An we will proudly pass them by
As we gae tae the shearin.

Chorus

An when the shearin is aa dune
We'll hae some ranting, roarin fun;
We'll hae some ranting, roarin fun
An forget the toils o the shearin.

Chorus

So bonnie lassie, fresh and fair,
Will ye be mine for ever mair?
Gin ye'll be mine, syne I'll be thine,
And we'll gang nae mair tae the shearin.

Jamie Telfer O The Fair Dodheid

I'm Jamie Telfer o the Fair Dodheid And a harried man am I;
There's nocht left at the Fair Dodheid But a greetin wife and bairnies three.

I'm Jamie Telfer o the Fair Dodheid
And a harried man am I;
There's nocht left at the Fair Dodheid
But a greetin wife and bairnies three.

Warn Wat o Harden an his men
And gar them ride Borthwick water wide;
Warn Gowdilands an Allenhaugh
An Gilmanscleuch an Commonside.

As he passed the yett o Preisthaughswire
He warned the Currers o the Lea,
An as ye cam doon the Hermitage slack
Warn doughty Willie o Gorrenberry.

Green Grows The Laurels

♩ = 138

A yince had a true love but now A hae nane

An now since she left me I'll bide my lane;

An now since she left me con - ten - ted I'll be

For I'll find a - no - ther where ev - er she be.

chorus:

Green grows the lau - rels and so does the yew,

Sor - ry was I when I part - ed with you;

But at our next meet - ing A hope you'll prove true,

And we'll turn owre the lau - rels tae the reid, white and blue.

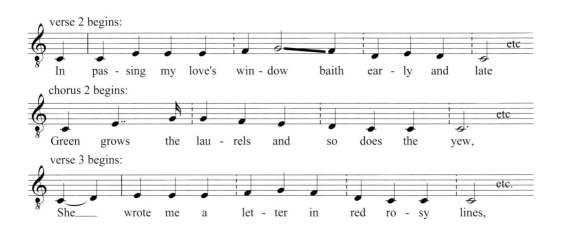

verse 2 begins:

In pas - sing my love's win - dow baith ear - ly and late   etc

chorus 2 begins:

Green grows the lau - rels and so does the yew,   etc

verse 3 begins:

She___ wrote me a let - ter in red ro - sy lines,   etc.

A yince had a true love but now A hae nane
An now since she left me I'll bide my lane;
An now since she left me contented I'll be
For I'll find another where ever she be.

Chorus
Green grows the laurels and so does the yew,
Sorry was I when I parted with you;
But at our next meeting A hope you'll prove true,
An we'll turn owre the laurels tae the reid, white, and blue.

In passing my love's window baith early and late
The looks she takes at me my heart it doth ache;
The looks she takes at me if many would kill
She's the lass o the innocent and the lass I lo'e still.

Chorus

She wrote me a letter in red rosy lines,
A wrote her an answer all twisted and twined;
Saying you keep your love letters and I'll keep mine,
And if you write to your love, I'll write tae mine.

Chorus

The Wild Colonial Boy

verse 2 and all subsequent verses begin:

Twas of a wild colonial boy Jack Donal was his name,
His poor, but honest parents wis born at Castlemaine;
He was his father's favourite son his mother's only joy,
Alas their cares and sorrows wis the wild colonial boy.

At hammer throwing Jack wis guid and throwing a command;
He led the boys in all his pride from dusk till early dawn.
At fishing or at poaching trout he was the real McCoy,
How dearly all the neighbours loved the wild colonial boy.

Twas at the age of sixteen when he left his native home,
And through Australia soon he roved, bush ranging he did roam;
He struck the beach with Meludge ship and robbed Lord Nichol Roy
And trembling he gave up the goal, to the wild colonial boy.

Twas at the age of thirty when he joined his wild career
And when he saw no stranger, no danger did he fear;
He robbed the lonely squire and his flocks he did destroy,
And a terror tae Australia wis the wild colonial boy.

"It's come along my heartress we'll rove the mountains high,
Together we will plunder, together we will die;
It's we'll ride over mountains and we'll ride over plains,
Or soon be brought to slavery bound down by iron chains."

When Jack arose next morning and slowly rode along,
Listening to the mocking birds with pleasant loving song;
He saw three mounted troopers, Kelly, Davis, and Fitzroy;
They all rode up to capture him, the wild colonial boy.

"Surrender now Jack Donal for ye see there's three to one,
Surrender in the King's name sir, for you are a plundering son;"
He pulled a pistol from his belt and waved that little toy,
"I'll fight but not surrender," cried the wild colonial boy.

He fired at trooper Kelly and brought him to the ground,
And turning round to Davis he received a deadly wound;
While bathing in his youthful blood he fired at Fitzroy
And this is how they captured him, the wild colonial boy.

The Lads That Were
Reared Amang Heather

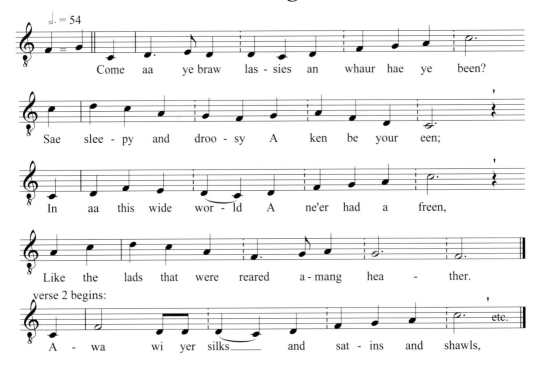

Come aa ye braw lassies an whaur hae ye been?
Sae sleepy and droosy A ken be your een;
In aa this wide world A ne'er had a freen,
Like the lads that were reared amang heather.

Awa wi yer silks and satins and shawls,
Yer soirees and concerts and fashionable balls;
For a dance in the barn is worth ten in the halls,
Wi the lads that were reared amang heather.

Take a walk doon oor cities grand buildings ootside,
And they boast o the days that we spent in oor pride;
And aa the big ships that were built on the Clyde
By the lads that were reared amang heather.

When a King wants guid sodgers he kens whaur tae send
Wi their bonnets and plaidies frae mountain and glen;
And their brave loyal heroes there none can defend
Like the lads that were reared amang heather.

The world famed Burns, Tom Campbell, and Scott;
Tannahill, Willie Penman, shall ne'er be forgot;
And Archie MacAllister frae auld Killie's nook,
Were the lads that were reared amang heather.

The lads that were reared amang the heather: Willie with his brothers, Sandy, Tom and Jock. Photographed at Hawick in 1916.

Bloody Waterloo

As a lady was a-walkin alang the banks o Clyde,

The tears ran doon her rosy cheeks as I passed by her side;

I saw her bosom heavin, her voice was low and true

She wis weepin for her Willie lad, who sailed for Waterloo.

As a soldier was a-walking, he did a fair maid spy,

He says, "My love, what aileth thee? thy bosom doth heave high."

"I've lost my ain dear Willie, the lad I do lo'e true,

An A hanna heard frae Willie since he sailed for Waterloo."

"What were the marks your Willie wore?" the soldier did enquire,

"He wore a Hielan bonnet, a feather standin high;

His big broadsword hung by his side and his dark suit so true,

These were the marks my Willie wore when he sailed for Waterloo."

"I was your Willie's comrade, I saw your Willie die:
Six bay'net wounds were in his sides afore he doon wad lie.
Then holdin up his hand he cried, 'Some Frenchman's slain me noo!'
It was I that closed your Willie's eyes on bloody Waterloo."

"O Willie, dearest Willie!" – and she could say no more,
She flung herself in the soldier's arms while she thus the tidings bore;
"Death open wide your jaws and swallow me up too
For Willie lies among the slain on bloody Waterloo."

"Stand up, stand up, my fair maid, my dearest, do not frown!"
An flingin off his grey coat, his tartans they hung down;
His big broadsword hung by his side and his dark suit sae true,
"I am your ain dear Willie lad who sailed for Waterloo."

"Stand up, stand up, my fair maid, my dearest, do not frown!"
An flingin off his grey coat, his tartans they hung down;
"Now since we've met we ne'er shall pairt, till death shall us divide,
And hand in hand in wedlock bands alang the banks o Clyde."

Sons O Bonnie Scotland

♩ = 92

Oh let aa— the rhy-mers sing A-boot the lands_ both far and near,

My_ voice I'll raise and sing in praise My na-tive land sae dear:

Whaur grows the bon-nie hea-ther bells Blithe burn-ies rush-ing clear

That_ roll a-mang the braes_ o bon-nie_ Scot-land.

chorus: N.B. extra stresses in first line

It's the land_whaur he-roes fought and fell, the land whaur bon-nie las-sies dwell

Whaur grows the bon-nie hea-ther bells a-mang the braes_ o Scot-land.

It's the land we boast a-boot wi pride Sur-roun-ded by____the o-cean wide

Whae was it fa-mous made the Clyde? But the sons o bon nie_ Scot-land.

O let aa the rhymers sing
Aboot the lands both far and near,
My voice I'll raise and sing in praise
My native land sae dear:
Whaur grows the bonnie heather bells,
Blithe burnies rushing clear
That roll amang the braes
O bonnie Scotland.

Chorus

It's the land whaur heroes fought and fell;
The land whaur bonnie lassies dwell,
Whaur grows the bonnie heather bells
Amang the braes o Scotland;
It's the land we boast aboot wi pride
Surrounded by the ocean wide,
Whae was it famous made the Clyde?
But the sons o bonnie Scotland.

O whaur is the Scotchman
Wudnae feel patriotic fire,
When he sings aboot the bards
That have strung the Doric lyre;
Oor herts with mirth and happiness,
Oor souls they did inspire
When they sung aboot
Oor country bonnie Scotland.

Chorus

The Soldier's Return

air: The Lea Rig

When owre yon hills the bullets flew
The shells they burst like fury o;
When doon yon trench in single file
We ran like hell my dearie o.
Doon by the burn where Swiss trench lies
The nicht was dark and dreary o,
An mony's the lad nae rise again
Nae mair he'll see his dearie o.

But when the word 'advance' was passed
Oor eyes wi sleep were bleary o;
We sang the 'marshallease' o France
But *Scotland Yet* my dearie o.
Nae doubt the folk at hame wud mourn
For gallant lads sae cheerie o,
But when Germans fell like sheaves o corn
We thocht of you my dearie o.

When owre yon seas we'll come again
And war nae mair my dearie o;
And you and I are aa oor ain
We'll drink a cup sae cheerie o.
And in auld Edinburgh toon
We'll name the day my dearie o;
An we like bairnies cuddle doon,
We hae nae cause tae weary o.

The Wag At The Waa

A've been hae'in a so-cia-ble nicht   Wi my cro-nies a so-cia-ble crew,

Oh A've had a drink twa or more or less,   And A be-gin tae su-spect that I'm fu!

A'm no ve-ry sure whaur I am   A'm rai-ther the waur o the drap-pie

It's a quar-ter tae twa, the last bus is a-wa,   What does't mat-ter as long as A'm hap-py.

chorus:

She's wat-chin the wag at the waa,   Cro-nies A'll hae tae be lea-vin,___

My con-science, a quar-ter tae twa   An A said A'd be hame at e-lee-ven;___

So cro-nies guid-nicht tae ye   aa,   Losh but I'm sweir tae gae 'wa,

But Mis-tress Mc Cann's Wai-tin up for her man   And she's wat-chin the wag at the waa.

77

A've been hae'in a sociable nicht
Wi my cronies a sociable crew;
Oh A've had a drink twa more or less,
And A begin tae suspect that I'm fu!
A'm no very sure whaur I am,
A'm raither the waur o the drappie;
It's a quarter tae twa, the last bus is awa,
What does't matter as lang as A'm happy,

> *Chorus*
> She's watchin the wag at the waa
> Cronies A'll hae tae be leavin;
> My conscience, a quarter tae twa,
> An A said A'd be hame at eleeven.
> So cronies guid-nicht tae ye aa,
> Losh, but I'm sweir tae gae 'wa,
> But Mistress McCann's
> Waitin up for her man
> And she's watchin the wag at the wa.

When A meet wi they cronies o mine,
And we've had a drammie or twa;
When the time comes tae pairt,
Man it gangs tae ma hairt,
It's a thocht tae gang hame throw the snaw.
When a pal puts his airm roon ma neck,
And implores me tae bide a while langer,
If he prigs wi me sair, "It's the wife," A declare,
"A wid stop but for fear o her anger."

> *Chorus*

Owre The Muir Amang The Heather

Comin through the craigs o Kyle
Amang the bonnie, blooming heather,
There I met a bonnie lassie
Keepin aa her yowes thegither.

Chorus
Owre the muir amang the heather,
Owre the muir amang the heather,
There I met a bonnie lassie
Keepin aa her yowes thegither.

Says I, "My lass whaur dae ye gang
Sae fer awa frae ony ither?"
Says she, "My faither's far frae hame,
And I'm keepin aa his yowes thegither."

Chorus

We laid us doon upon a bank
Sae warm and sunny was the weather;
And as we lay she sang a sang,
Till echoes rang a mile and ferther,

Chorus

She charmed my hairt and aye sinsyne
I could nae think on ony ither:
By sea and sky, she shall be mine,
The bonnie lass amang the heather

Chorus

The Bonnie Wee Trampin Lass

As A gaed oot yin Sat-ur-day nicht for tae hae a wee bit stroll,—

Ne'er think-ing how the time was flyin till A gaed by the toll;—

A ha-d-na far gane by— the toll the Car-ters mill to pass,

When whae dae ye think A chanced to meet? but a bon-nie wee tram-pin lass.—

chorus:

"Oh whaur are ye gaun, oh gie me yer haun, and hoo are ye daein?" says I—

"Haud up yer heid me bonnie wee lass, and din-na look sae shy;—

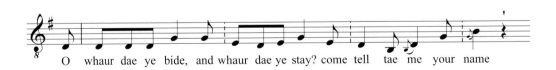

O whaur dae ye bide, and whaur dae ye stay? come tell tae me your name

And wud yer fai-ther be ang-ry, if A wis tae set ye hame?"

As I gaed oot yin Saturday nicht for tae hae a wee bit stroll,
Ne'er thinking how the time was flyin till A gaed by the toll;
A hadna far gane by the toll the Carters mill to pass,
When whae dae ye think A chanced to meet? but a bonnie wee trampin lass.

Chorus
"Oh whaur are ye gaun, oh gie me yer haun, and hoo are ye daein?" says I
"Haud up yer heid me bonnie wee lass, and dinna look sae shy;
Oh whaur dae ye bide, and whaur dae ye stay? Come tell tae me yer name
And wud yer faither be angry if A wis tae set ye hame?"

She said she wis working doon in yon Carters mill,
Winding hanks o yarn ye ken, she liked it awfu weel;
She only had ten bob a week, she hadna been on fu time,
Says I "Me lass take care of that, for you'll very soon be mine.

Chorus

We stood there bletherin for a while, aboot that thing caad love,
Ne'er thinking how the time was flying till the skies grew dark above;
She drew her shawl aroon her heid and to me she did exclaim,
"I say young man it's getting late and time that we were hame."

Chorus

But now since we've got mairried, we're as happy as can be,
Twa bonnie bairnies by me side, and a third yin on me knee;
When e'er we gan oot for a stroll the Carters mill tae pass,
A think o the happy times A've hed, since A met wi the trampin lass.

Chorus

Mistress Paxton's Shop

Mistress Paxton keeps a shop,
She sells baith cheap and dear things;
And mony a usefu thing she keeps,
And faith she has some queer things.

I daundered in the other night,
Tae buy a cake o blackin;
An tuik a guid look roon the shop
The time that we sat crackin.

Sae here I hae them merkit doon,
An if ye'll pay attention,
The names o aathing in the shop,
I carefully will mention.

There was bacca, saip and carpet shoon,
Screw nails and bakin soda;
And senna leaves a usefu thing,
For ony no weel body.

Fuses, lampwicks and nebcloot nails,
Split peas an fiddle rosit;
An castor oil there's plenty there,
If ony wants a dose o't.

Whings, biscuits, birdseed, elshun hefts,
Cork soles and apple jelly;
Spunks, treacle, ham and question buiks,
Preens, caraway seeds and keely.

Stairch, ink and dandelion peels,
Clock oil and sugarallie;
Tam Newton sooks a lot o that,
He has the caul puir fella.

Snuff, galace buttons, soda scones,
Thread, reddin kames and gundy;
An paper collars, usefu things
For Saturday or Sunday.

Eggs, gimlets, marmalade and tape,
Hair oil and pepper boxes;
And things for gaun roon weemens' necks.
Gie like the tails o foxes.

Whups, whitin, slater nails and saut,
Fit rules and leather mittens;
Pot barley, salts and sparrables,
An things for haudin spittins.

Spoke shaves, hymnbuiks and turpentine,
An gutta percha slippers;
Magnesia, studs and potted heid,
An twa three pairs o nippers.

Pipe covers, thrawcraiks and testaments,
Rice, vinegar and tackits;
Glue, parritch sticks and corn floor,
Rowed up in tipenny packets.

Fish, lead-drops, corks and sharpin stanes,
Queensheads and yellow ochre;
Saltpetre, shears and sticks o rock,
As lang as ony poker.

Spoons, spectacles and lots o cheese,
American and gowdies;
A new machine for smeeking bees,
An traps for catchin mowdies.

Boots, floor-pots, gum and galaces
Steel pens and stickin plaister,
Elastic pumps wad gar ye jump,
Like ony dancin maister.

New fashioned stuff for drawing teeth,
Ye never find the pain o't;
If I had ony teeth tae draw
I'd buy a half a stane o't.

It suits the purpose unco weel,
An lots o folk are buyin't;
We got some fun the ither nicht,
When Geordie Luke was tryn't.

He put a pickle in his mooth,
Tae see how it affectit;
But faith it ackit in a way
That Geordie no expectit

It bade a while in his mooth,
An then began a fizzin;
An then it made a noise as if,
A thousand bees were bizzin.

But faith, I think I've said eneuch
Its time that I was drappin;
Ma papers getting near a close
An ten o'clock is chappin.

Willie and Frances Scott with three of their family,
Sandy, Thomas and Dougie
(from left to right) in 1944.

shepherd's counting system

Yan	Sithere	Yanadict	Yana bumfit
Tan	Hithere	Tanadict	Tana bumfit
Tithere	Hathere	Setheredict	Sethere bumfit
Mithere	Dathere	Metheredict	Methere bumfit
Fimf	Dict	Bumfit	Gigit

Sheep being driven to the Auction Mart through old Hawick and down Noble Place, Hawick, about 1912.

The Shepherd's Song

I'm a shep-herd and I rise ere the sun is in the skies,

I can lamb the yowes wi o - ny o them aa;

An I like my flock to feed, an look fresh and fair in - deed,

But I wish the cauld east winds would ne - ver blaw.

chorus:

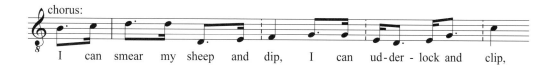

I can smear my sheep and dip, I can ud-der - lock and clip,

I can lamb the yowes wi o - ny o them aa:

I can par - rock, I can twin, aye, an cheat them wi a skin,

But I wish the cauld east winds would ne - ver blaw.

I'm a shepherd and I rise ere the sun is in the skies,
I can lamb the yowes wi ony o them aa;
An I like my flock to feed, an look fresh and fair indeed,
But I wish the cauld east winds would never blaw.

Chorus

I can smear my sheep and dip, I can udderlock and clip,
I can lamb the yowes wi ony o them aa;
I can parrock, I can twin, aye, an cheat them wi a skin,
But I wish the cauld east winds would never blaw.

When the winter time is here, for their lives I sometimes fear
Tae some sheltered nook my flock I'll gently caa;
Or in the morning grey, I'll turn them tae the brae,
Or seek them mang the tooring wreaths o snaw.

Chorus

In the lambing time I wot, it was little sleep I got,
But when the summer's sunny breezes blaw;
On yon bonnie hill, I'll lie and sleep my fill
When the lambs are runnin roon aboot me braw.

Chorus

I can cut and merk, and spean, or drive them to the train,
Though their dams be rinnin bleatin in a raw;
A can stand the merket through, and richt well A sell them too,
And my maister's money safely bring it aa.

Chorus

I can work in time o need, I can sow or hoe or weed;
I can swing the scythe wi ony o them aa;
I can cut the corn and bin, and richt braw stooks leave behin
That will stand the autumn winds when hooses faa.

Chorus

And when I've done my wark, though the nicht be e'er sae dark,
At a swaggering step I'll hie mysel awa
To the lassie, dearest yin, she's the best aneath the sun –
An she'll name the day we'll be nae langer twa.

Chorus

Now my neebor herds beware when ye gang to show or fair,
The fiery liquor never taste ava;
Juist thoule your drouth awee, till your ain braw hills ye'll see,
And the bonnie bubblin streams will quell it aa.

Chorus

Lambing Time

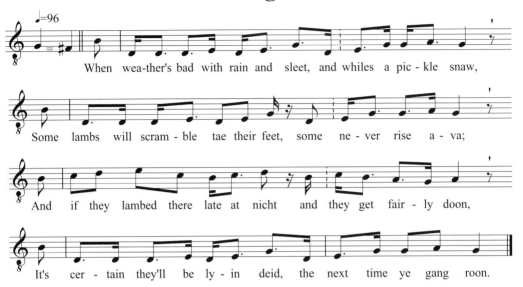

When weather's bad with rain and sleet, and whiles a pickle snaw,
Some lambs will scramble tae their feet, some never rise ava;
And if they lambed there late at nicht and they get fairly doon,
It's certain they'll be lyin deid, the next time ye gang roon.

Never fret in lambing time when things may whiles gang wrang,
Twin up your yowes that hae got milk as fer's your twins 'll gang;
And after that there's nothing for't but caa the waafs away,
Just draw the keel stick owre their rump, it's aught that ye can dae.

And hanging too taks place at times in some dry shelterd nook,
And herds will get their patience tried wi lambs that winna sook;
And gimmer beasts that's scarce o milk, they are the deils tae twin,
And herds are often unco glad to get their sheep shed in.

You seldom get a lambing throw without a drooning turn,
The yowes are bleating on the braes, the lambs swept doon the burn;
Dinna, if their gimmers fret, ye needna grudge them sair,
For mebbe in another year she'll lamb an nurse a pair.

And foxes tae will tak a wheen especially when yin's thrang;
For it's only nature's instinct they prepare to feed their young;
Though they be dirty stinking brutes you must admire the strain
That bred a beast so devilish cute with sharp and cunning brain.

Ewe and her lamb. Willie worked most of his life with black-faced sheep. The lamb
was exhibited at all the big shows; as a lamb, a gimmer and a full-grown ewe.
"She was never beaten."

If ever you come to Irvine don't try to buck the law

You'll find that they are sharper than a newly made hacksaw;

Especially the constable that's known as "Dipper Jim"

You can bet your last three halfpence - there aint no flies on him.

Buff Wilson

Dandie

Leading the peat stacks, Windshielknowe 1939,
with his young sons Sandy and Douglas.

Come in ahint, ye wanderin tyke
Did ever a body see yer like?
Wha learnt ye aa thae poacher habits?
Come in ahint, ne'er heed the rabbits.
Noo bide there, or I'll warm yer lug!
My certie, caa yersel a dug?
Noo owre the dyke, an through the park
Let's see if ye can dae some wark!
Way wide there, yont the burn's bank;
Get roon aboot them, watch the gap.
Hey Dandie, haud them frae the slap!
Ye've got them noo, that's no sae bad:
Noo bring them in, guid lad, guid lad.

Noo tak them canny owre the knowe;
Hey Dandie, kep that mawkit yowe.
The tither ane, hey - lowse yer grip!
The yowe, ye foumart, no the tip.
Ay, that's the ane - guid dog, guid dog.
Noo haud, hey canny, dinna tug.
She's mawkit bad, aye shair's I'm born;
We'll hae tae dip a wheen the morn.
Noo haud yer wheest, ye yelpin randie,
An dinna fricht them, daft dog Dandie.
He's owre the dyke - the Deil be in't!
Ye wanderin tyke, come in ahint.

Willie Scott's version of a poem by
W. D. Cocker

The Waddin O McPhee

air: Loch Lomond

At mony sprees I've been, but the best I've ever seen
Was held high up on Ben Lomond;
Every yin got fu, it was like a Waterloo
At the waddin o McPhee on Ben Lomond.
Some cam up the high road , some cam up the low road,
An some o them got lost in the gloamin;
An them that bide awa, they wernae there at aa
At the waddin o McPhee on Ben Lomond.

The minister got lost and we searched for him of course;
We searched high and low in the gloamin;
We found him on the hill, in his hand he held a gill
At the waddin o McPhee on Ben Lomond.
They kicked him up the high road, they kicked him up the low road
And somebody kicked his abdomen;
Afore he gaed awa, he said he wished he'd never saw
The waddin o McPhee on Ben Lomond.

Then we had a feed, we had pies and pottie heid,
Bannocks stacked high in the morning;
We'd the rump o a coo and the leg o a cushie doo
At the waddin o McPhee on Ben Lomond.
Some gaed hame the high road, and some gaed hame the low road
And some o them got lost in the gloamin;
But the bridegroom and the bride were cremated side by side
High up on the hill on Ben Lomond.

An Awfa Chap For Fun

A'm an awfa chap for fun, my name is Geordie Dunn,

And if you saw me through and through, you'd think the very same;

My faither was afore me, a reg'lar jolly one,

An A'm just a chip off the real old block, for A'm aye sae fu o fun.

Chorus

A'm an awfa chap for fun, A'm a deil an aa for fun,

For A never met wi my equal yet, I was aye sae fu of fun.

As A gaed daunerin doon the street, ae nicht sae fresh and fair,
I met a great big bouncin lass wi bonnie ginger hair;
Sae politely A addressed her, A says, "My dearest yin,
A wish yer Granny saw ye, for A'm aye sae fu o fun."

Chorus

A took her tae a sweetie shop, no far across the way,
A saw her teeth was waterin, and A asked her what she'd hae?
She whispered kindly in my ear, "Your pleisure, Geordie Dunn,"
A says, "We'll hae a dauner then, for A'm aye sae fu o fun."

Chorus

As we gaed daunerin doon the street, I chanced tae speak o love,
I threw my airms aroun her waist, says I, "My turtle dove,
O how A wish you were for sale, some sixteen pence a pund
A'd buy some eichteen stane o you, and mak ye Mistress Dunn."

Chorus

But noo, since we got mairrit, she has proved a scolding wife,
And if ever A offend her, she's like to take my life;
She kicks my shins and pulls my hair, and thraws me tae the grun,
But I just return the compliments, for A'm aye sae fu o fun.

Chorus

Piper MacNeil

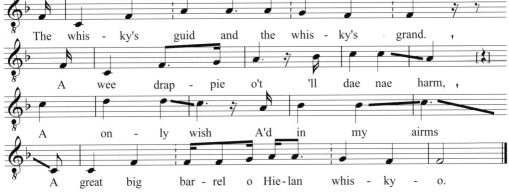

Ye'll aa hae heard o Piper MacNeil
A canty chap and a coothie chiel,
And aa my days A loed him weel
For he dearly loed the whisky o.

Chorus

    The whisky's guid and the whisky's grand,
    A wee drappie o't'll dae nae harm,
    A only wish A'd in my airms
    A great big barrel o Hielan whisky o.

When A cam staggerin hame yin nicht
As fu as ony man could be,
A struck a post an doon A fell,
Juist wi a wee drap whisky o.

    Chorus

When A cam staggerin tae the door
Me mither rase an she slipped the bar;
But when she saw ma claes aa glar
She said, "Curse tae the Hielan whisky o."

Chorus

"Noo mither ye neednae angry be,
Nor in a passion ye neednae flee;
For aye until the day A dee
A'll aye tak a wee drap whisky o."

    Chorus

My Hielan Hame

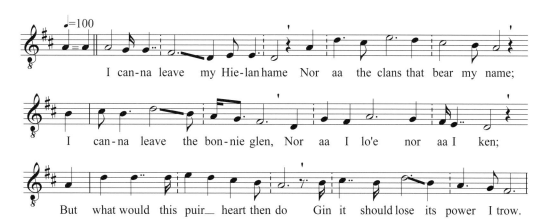

I canna leave my Hielan hame
Nor aa the clans that bear my name;
I canna leave the bonnie glen,
Nor aa I lo'e nor aa I ken;
But what would this puir heart then do
Gin it should lose its power I trow.

Chorus

Flowers may bloom fer ayont the sea
But oh, my Hielan hame for me.

My faither sleeps beneath the sod
My mither shares his cauld abode;
Yon sunny shieling on the brae
Hae oft heard sounds of grief and wae;
And I its tenant left alane,
Lamenting o'er my Hielan hame.

Chorus

They tell me I'll get wealth and ease
Wi nocht tae vex but aa tae please;
They tell me I'll get gold and fame
They tempt me wi a glorious name;
But what can aa their wealth impart
To me wha has a broken heart?

Chorus

Each flower that blooms on foreign fell
Would mind me o my heather bell;
Each little streamlet, nook, or turn,
Would mind me o Glenorick's burn;
How can I leave a scene so dear,
Without a sigh, without a tear?

Chorus

The Yella Haired Laddie

The maidens are smiling in rocky Glencoe;
The clansmen are arming to rush on the foe,
Gay banners are streaming as forth leads the clan,
And the yella haired laddie is first in the van.

The pibroch is kindlin their hearts in the war,
The Cameron slogan is heard from afar;
They close for the struggle where many shall fall
But the yella haired laddie is foremost of all.

He tow'rs on the waves like the wild rolling tide,
No kinsmen of Evans shall stand by his side;
The Camerons gather around him alone
He heeds not the danger and fear is unknown.

The plumes of his bonnet are seen through the fight,
The beacons of valour they light with the sight;
He saw not yon claymore each a traitrous thrust
And the sound of the coronach comes on the gale.

The maidens are crying in rocky Glencoe;

There's gloom in the valley at sunrise will go.

No sun can the gloom from our hearts chase away,

For the yellow-haired laddie lies cauld in the clay.

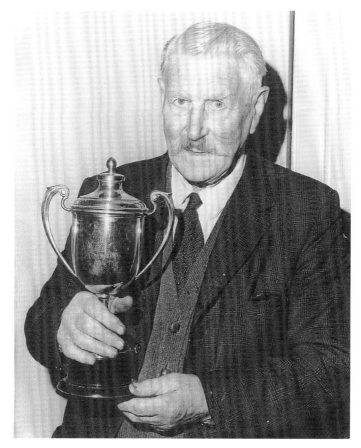

With the TMSA cup for Traditional Singing.

Bonnie Jeannie Shaw

Oh A'm fer frae bon - nie Scot -land, nae a lov-in yin is here,

A din - na see the auld folk, the folk A love sae dear;

A'll__ leave this for -eign land with__ scenes and sights sae braw,

And A'll wan - der back tae Scot - land and my Bonnie Jean nie Shaw.

chorus:

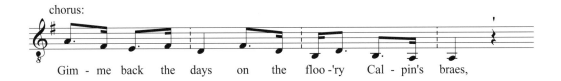

Gim - me back the days on the floo -'ry Cal - pin's braes,

And the bon - nie las - sie I love best of aa;

I would cross the o - cean wide, for to wan - der by the Clyde

In the gloam - in, wi my bon - nie Jean - nie Shaw.

100

Oh A'm fer frae bonnie Scotland, nae a lovin yin is here,

A dinna see the auld folk, the folk A love sae dear;

A'll leave this foreign land with scenes and sights sae braw,

And A'll wander back tae Scotland and my bonnie Jeannie Shaw.

Chorus

Gimme back the days on the flooery Calpin's braes,

And the bonnie lassie I love the best of aa;

I would cross the ocean wide, for to wander by the Clyde

In the gloamin, wi my bonnie Jeannie Shaw.

A dinna see the thistle, nor the heather on the hill,

A dinna hear the mavis sing its fairly fill;

My heart with pure delight sae up an gang awa,

To be home in dear auld Scotland and my bonnie Jeanie Shaw.

Chorus

John Reilly

I had an old companion boys,
John Reilly was his name;
In fair or stormy weather boys
John Reilly's just the same:
His heart was like the mountain boys,
His honour you could try,
And when he'd any money boys,
John Reilly's always dry.

    Chorus
    O Bass's ale, Bass's ale,
    By the pail, by the pail,
    He would order Susanna to go out
    and buy Dublin stout, Dublin stout,
    He would shout, he would shout
    "Keep drinking boys, never say dry"
    O whisky bright, whisky bright,
    Gin and wine, gin and wine;
    He would pull down the bottle
    And then he would cry
    "Mary Ann fill your can
    For your honour John Reilly is dry."

Now early every morning boys
When he gets out of bed,
There is no feathered bolster boys
Lies 'neath old Reilly's head;
And when the sun begins to shine
So eager and so sly,
He slips out for a bucket boys,
Old Reilly's always dry.

    Chorus

His mother often told him boys,
When he was but a youth,
That all the other Reilly boys
Had died of whisky drouth;
It is a sad misfortune boys
And no one can deny,
That with his elbow bending boys,
John Reilly's always dry.

    Chorus

Jock Geddes And The Soo

Jock Geddes on some business bent
Tae mairket yae day gaed licht-hairtit;
His mither, carefu o her son,
Saw Jock fu frig ere he depairtit,
For Jock at mairket whiles got fu
The place where scamps were there tae tak him
And so his mither at the door cries,
"Come hame sober, Jock, ye nickum!"

Chorus
Braw, braw to bey weel likit,
Braw, braw to bey sae bonnie;
Owre weel likit winna dae –
Sae muckle thocht on bey sae mony.

But Jock as yaisual suin forgot
The plain injunctions o his mither;
The mairket made him awfa dry -
The cyair was whisky, deil anither!
He met a freen as dry's himsel
An awa they went to weet their wezans;
Glass efter glass they drank until –
The total number cam to dizens.

Chorus

Jock rase at last an made for hame,

He hedna taen his mother's biddin;

He couldna thrive – he tripped an fell

Wi aa his length alang the midden

Jock juist lay still, fell fast asleep;

The drink had fairly stopped his kickin;

The soo cam by an smelt his moo

An likin that, commenced the lickin!

Chorus

Th'enormous soo still lickit on

Cries Jock, "Noo, Jean, haud aff, that's plenty!

Let Kirsty hae a smack or twa,

For A'm shair ye hae haen mair than twenty!

For A ken A'm a weel forked chiel

But dinna get in sic a swather;

I'll let ye kiss me, but dods sake

Ye needna eat me aa thegither."

Chorus

At last his sober sense came roon

An lookin up saw Sandy Cam'ell;

"Ye muckle, nesty, ugly brute,

Nae mair upon me will ye wammle!"

Jock rase an spat for near an oor,

The soo had played an awfu plisky!

The pig was killed that very next day,

An Jock has niver since taen whisky.

Chorus

Braw, braw, to bey weel likit,

Braw, braw it is, but bless me,

Owre weel likit, winna dae

A never thocht a soo would kiss me!

Scotch Medley

Gae bring ma guid auld herp yince mair, Gae bring it free and fast;

O aa the airts the wind can blaw Tis me-mory of the past;

For Wul-lie brewed a peck o malt wi auld John Bar-ley-corn;

Then steer me back to E-rin's Isle For I'm a Scotch-man born.

Then steer me back to E-rin's Isle For I'm a Scotch-man born.

Gae bring ma guid auld herp yince mair,

Gae bring it free and fast;

O aa the airts the wind can blaw

Tis memory of the past;

For Wullie brewed a peck o malt

Wi auld John Barleycorn;

Then steer me back to Erin's Isle

For I'm a Scotchman born.

Then steer me back to Erin's Isle

For I'm a Scotchman born.

The heath waves wild upon the hill

Far across the sea;

Then let me like a soldier fall

Beside the rowan tree;

There was a lad was born in Kyle

When comin through the rye;

"O Jane, O Jane my pretty Jane,

Goodbye, sweetheart goodbye.

O Jane, O Jane my pretty Jane,

Goodbye, sweetheart goodbye."

The thistle wags upon the field
John Anderson my Jo;
I dreamt a dream, a happy dream,
Doon by the Ohio;
"Oh Minnie wilt thou gang wi me?"
Cries Jock o Hazeldean;
Ma mither ment my auld breeks
Doon by yon auld mill stream.
Ma mither ment my auld breeks
Doon by yon auld mill stream.

Then sing tae me the auld Scotch sangs,
 I'll row thee owre the Clyde;
The standards on the Braes o Mar
And I'll wait till the turn o the tide;
For gloomy winter's noo awa
In Morag's fairy glen;
"Get up auld wife and bar the door
For noo it's half past ten.
Get up, auld wife and bar the door
For noo it's half past ten."

Killiebank Braes

The beams of the setting sun yellow were gleaming

O'er Aitken's high summit where lambkins did play;

A mist of bright flies owre Meggit were dancing

And slowly retreating the night clouds of day.

Weel rowed in my plaidie and carelessly skipping,

And crooning a sang for to shorten the way;

At last I spied bonnie Nancy come tripping

Amang the green breckens, on Killiebank Braes.

Bareheided and barfit, as licht as a fairy,

O, had ye but seen how she trippit alang;

My heart it lap licht at the sicht o my dearie,

I ran oot to meet her, yon breckens amang.

Says I, "Bonnie Nancy, o whaur are ye gaun

And what are ye seekin sae late here, I say?"

She laughing replied, "If ye are annoyed,

I'm seekin the kye here on Killiebank Braes."

Says I, "I'll gang wi ye." says she, "But ye wunna."

Says I, "But I wull," says she, "I say no."

"Weel weel, then," says I, "If gang wi ye I mauna,

A kiss I maun hae, and that instantly tae."

I grasped her and kissed her, and squeezed and caressed her,

She up and miscaaed me and bade me gae awa,

She frowned and she smiled and caaed me a plague,

And whuppit me lugs weel, on Killiebank Braes.

Bonnie Tyneside

Bonnie Tyneside I see thee once more

After long years of absence away from thy shore;

In far distant countries a rambler I've been

Much have I suffered and much I have seen.

I've lived in the lands where the sun brighter shone,

But I ne'er saw a country as fair as my own;

I never have seen in my wanderings wide

A spot I like better than Bonnie Tyneside.

Bonnie Tyneside where my infancy passed

Like a beautiful dream too pleasant to last;

I see the green fields where in youth I have strayed

And the auld school at Wall where oft times I've played.

The school master still in the village is seen;

And the school children still are at play on the green;

But the school mates of old they have gone far and wide

They've wandered away now from Bonnie Tyneside.

Bonnie Tyneside I come weary and worn,
Few are the friends left to greet my return;
I'll away to the hills and wander all day
Upon the green knowes where the lambs are at play.
The wiley old sheep know the tracks on the fells;
The bonnie wee birds have a home in the dells;
But a home and a hearth I have yet to provide
For now I'm a stranger on Bonnie Tyneside.

Bonnie Tyneside my loved one is here,
Awaiting my coming, my love to declare;
Through long years of absence she faithful has been,
Tho the wide ocean stood like a barrier between.
She's as pure as a morning in beautiful May
And as fresh as a rose on a Midsummer's day;
How happy I'll be with my love for a bride,
In a snug little cottage on Bonnie Tyneside.

The Kielder Hunt

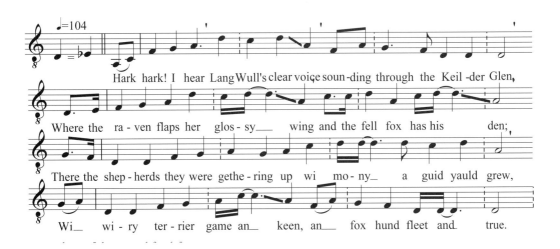

Hark hark! I hear Lang Wull's clear voice sounding through the Kielder Glen,

Where the raven flaps her glossy wing and the fell fox has his den;

There the shepherds they were gethering up wi mony a guid yauld grew,

Wi wiry terrier game an keen, an fox hund fleet and true.

Chorus

Hark away! Hark away!

O'er the bonnie hills of Kielder, Hark away!

There was Mowdie frae Emmethaugh, there was Royal frae Bakethinn;

There were hunds frae Reed and Kielder Heid, an Ruby by the Linn;

There were hunds of fame frae Irthingside, they try baith moss an crag;

Hark hark! That's Mowdie's loud clear note, he has bold Reynard's drag.

Chorus

Away an away, o'er hill and dale, an up by yonder Stell,
The music of the gallant pack resounds owre muir and dell;
See yon herd callant waves his plaid, list his loud tally-ho;
The fox is up and streaks away, o'er the edge o Hawkhope Flow.

Chorus

Hark forward, hark ye gallant hunds, hark onward hark away!
He kens the holes on Tosson Hills, he kens the holes at Rae;
There's no a den roon the Kale Stane but he kens weel I trow,
An aa the holes on Leriston, he kens them throw and throw.

Chorus

There's Wanny's Crags an Sewing Shiels and Christenbury too,
 Or if he win to Hareshaw Linn ye may bid him adieu;
The Key Heugh an the Cloven-Crags, the cove at Darna Haa
Chatlehope Spoots an the Wily holes, auld foxy kens them aa.

Chorus

Away an away owre bank an brae, they drive the wily game,
Where Mowdie, Ruby, Royal still uphaud their glorious fame;
See yon leish yald shepherd lads, how Monkside heights they climb,
They're the pride o aa the Borders wide, for wind and wiry limb.

Chorus

Throw yon wild glen they view him now right for the Yearning Linn,
By cairn an crag, o'er moss and hads, sae glorious was the din;
Weel dune! Hurrah! they've run him doon yon's Mowdie twirls him now,
The hunt is done, his brush is won I hear the death halloo.

Chorus

Then here's to Will o Emmethaugh, for he's a sportsman true,
Here's to Robbie o Bakethin an Rob o Keilder too;
At the Hopes Bewshaugh an Kersie Cleuch, Skaup Riggend an the Law;
In Tyne an Reed and Irthing heid, they're gallant sportsman aa.

Chorus

making and showing crooks

The Drouthie Driver

When the drouthie driver leaves his car and bends his elbow at the bar
Tae satisfy that urgent thirst tae see the motorist at 'is worst.
He thinks nae o the road aheid the road o mony maimt an deid
That drouthie drivers o the past is gruesome moniement hae cast.
O Dan, hed 'e no been sae thrawn an tried thy wife tae understan
She wasnae kickin up a fuss when she was at 'e tak the bus.
The nicht wore oan in drunken spree Dan widnae stop at twa'r three
Despite the plea o friendly barman "Ca canny Dan, 'e hae the car mun!".
The mair the barman hey persistit "Ach fill it up man" Dan insistit
"What atween the wife an you e'd thinkit wrang tae see is fu."

At length he left his drouthie brithers heedless o the life o ithers
The bletherin, blusterin, drunken chiel took his place ahint the wheel.
That fu, hey could hardley stand, but ahint the wheel he wis feelin grand,
Ey revved 'er up richt at his game and turnt her roun tae heid fur hame.
Past fifty, sixty, ay an mair, Dan prest his fit flat on the flair,
First ae side, syne the t'other a cursed menace aa thegither.
Out throw the nicht sae dark and dirty, ignored the limit sign o thirty
Hard gates an fences aa gat strewn an endless trail o wreck an ruin.
Noo ballin oot some auld Scots airs, the drunken demon oanward tears
Till sudden, wi a skreich o brakes, Dan to a shudderin standstill shakes.

A beardit chin an hornt heid, twa bluidshot een aa starin reid,
Glowerin at 'um frae among the whuns, Dan fair repentant o his sins.
O aa things that an earth do dwell Dan thocht is wis auld Nick himsel;
He left the car an lap the fence full regaint o sober sense.
Across the field at ilka sprint niver stopped tae look ahint
Or stoppt tae tak a braith till he wis hame at the hearth.
A wiser man noo herds his coos and taks the bus when he maun booze
A lick o paint hides aa the scars o broken gates and speeding cars.
But aa throw his official life, Dan daurna tell his faithful wife
That how it was he tore his coat he wis chased by Wida Wilkie's goat!

MacAlister Dances Before The King

Clansmen, the peats are burning bright, sit round then in a ring,
And I will tell of that great night I danced before the King.

For as a dancer in my youth, so great was my renown,
The King himself invited me to visit London town.

My brand new presentation kilt and ornaments I wore,
As with my skean-dhu I rapped upon the Palace door.

And soon I heard a lord or duke come running down the stairs,
Who to the keyhole put his mouth demanding who was there.

"Open the door," I sternly cried, "as quickly as you can,
Is this the way that you receive a Highland gentleman?"

The door was opened, word went round, "MacAlister is here"
And at this news the Palace rang with one tremendous cheer.

The King was sitting on his throne but down the steps he came,
Immediately the waiting lord pronounced my magic name.

The lovely ladies of the court with pearls and jewels decked,
All blushed and trembled as I bowed to them with great respect.

Slowly at first with hands on hips I danced with ease and grace,
Then raised me airms above me head and swifter grew the pace.

At last no human eye could see my steps so light and quick,
And from the floor great clouds of dust came rising fast and thick.

The King was deeply moved and shook me by the hand in friendship true,
"Alas," he cried. "Although a King, I canna dance like you."

And then the gracious Queen herself came smiling up to me,
She pinned a medal on my breast for everyone to see.

Her whisper I shall not forget nor how her eyes grew dim,
"Ah where were you MacAlister the day I married HIM?"

Performing at a
Burns supper
(1977).

Irthing Water Foxhounds

On the 'leev-enth of Oc-to-ber, eight-teen hun-dred and sev-en-ty three,

I will give you all par-ti-cu-lars if you'll lis-ten un-tae me:

The hounds frae Ir-thing Wa-ter an ap-point-ment to ful-fil

They cast a-way ower the Phi-la-shaws crags, bold Rey-nard's blood to spill.

chorus:

Tal-ly ho hark a-way! Tal-ly ho hark a-way!

Suc-cess to Ir-thing Wa-ter hounds O hark, hark a-way!

On the 'leeventh of October, eighteen hundred and seventy three,

I will give you all particulars if you'll listen untae me:

The hounds frae Irthing Water an appointment to fulfil

They cast away owre the Philashaws crags, bold Reynard's blood to spill.

Chorus

Tally ho hark away! Tally ho hark away!

Success to Irthing Water hounds

O hark, hark away!

At seven o'clock that morning they reached the Philashaws crags,
They sought the ground all over and couldn't find a drag;
Till the celebrated Mowdie he tried a favourite hole
He turned his head and to the pack, and loudly he did call.

Chorus

Now these hounds were called together, with speed I do declare,
And by they had a terrier, brought Reynard from the lair;
He did his best, he headed north but great to his surprise,
A female early in the field then darkened Reynard's eye.

Chorus

How gallantly those dogs run off they ran him to the spy;
With loud cries of vengeance that Reynard he should die;
The followers being far behind they thought their work was done,
But they met the hounds returning with two foxes instead of one.

Chorus

Now those animals they did their best, their precious blood to save,
And seeing that the race was run prepared for the grave;
Death was their fate they baith did own, dispute it if you can,
They killed a fox at the Philashaws crags and another at the Naked Man.

Chorus

Now we will drink success to the Irthing lads we will push the bottle round;
Owre lofty fells and mosses their melodious voices sound.
They are well known both far and near, for the hunting of the hounds,
From the Wellseas to Tynemouth Bar no better can be found.

Chorus

The Canny Shepherd Laddie O the Hills

♩=88 verse:

There's songs a-boot oor sol-diers and oor sai-lors by the score

of tin-kers and of tai-lors and of o-thers there's ga-lore,

But I'll sing to you a song_ that you've ne-ver heard be-fore

It's the can-ny shep-herd lad-die o the hills.

chorus:

Oh the shep-herds o the Co-quet, the Al-win and the Rede,

The Bow-mont and the Brea-mish, they're all the same_ breed;

Wi their col-lie dog be-side them and a stick with horn_ heid,

It's the can-ny shep-herd lad-die o the hills.

There's songs aboot oor soldiers and oor sailors by the score;
Of tinkers and of tailors and of others there's galore.
But I'll sing to you a song that you've never heard before
It's the canny shepherd laddie o the hills.

Chorus

Oh the shepherds o the Coquet, the Alwin and the Rede,
The Bowmont and the Breamish, they're all the same breed;
Wi their collie dog beside them and a stick with horn heid
It's the canny shepherd laddie o the hills.

They climb oot owre the mountain ere it's turned the break o day,
Through the bent and moss hags and round bogs they wend their way;
Quick to see a mawkit yin or a sheep that's strayed awa
It's the canny shepherd laddie o the hills.

Chorus

They send the collie aroond the sheep with a yell o "Gan oot wide"
Then whistle with the notes so shrill the dog drops in his stride;
"Come by Moss! doon in a bit I'll tak my stick oot owre yer hide"
It's the canny shepherd laddie o the hills.

Chorus

If the lambing time is stormy he will curse and he will swear,
There's a yowe that's lost its lamb and I've skinned an old yowe there;
Some o them have ta'en the sickness, nae mair trouble can I bear
It's the canny shepherd laddie o the hills.

Chorus

In the back-end tae the marts he'll gang if the prices they are dear,
To celebrate he'll treat his pals tae whisky and tae beer;
But if the prices they are bad, it taks a dram to cheer
The canny shepherd laddie o the hills.

    Chorus

In the winter when it's stormy and drifts are piling high,
He'll never flinch tae tak the risk that in the snow he may die;
His first care is his sheep are settled and sheltered safe may lie
The canny shepherd laddie o the hills.

    Chorus

At Alwinton they all turn oot tae see the Shepherds' Show;
Then in to Foremans for a drink they with their cronies go;
They'll argue and they'll sing and shout, but fecht? well bless me no,
The canny shepherd laddie o the hills.

    Chorus

Now if ye've gaun among them as A've done for forty years,
Nae kinder hairted folk you'll meet if you look far or near;
The kettle's set a boiling and they cry, "Sit you doon here"
The canny shepherd laddie o the hills.

    Chorus

A've said nae words aboot their wives, A'm shair there is no need,
But in every house I've been tae yet they seem to be the heid;
And I'm sure you'll all agree with me, it taks a hell of a good wife to breed
A canny shepherd laddie o this hills.

    Chorus

Willie worked at Hartwoodsmyre on the Wemyss estate (now the Buccleuch estate) from 1944 to 1953. With him (from left to right) Peter Outerson, ploughman; Marjory Jack, landgirl; Rob Outerson, assistant shepherd; Willie Scott, herd; Willie McFarlane, farmer's son and POW (name unknown).

Herd Laddie O The Glen

O when A was a lad-die A leived up a glen

A wis lear - ning tae herd wi twae auld bear - ded men,

The__ ques - tions they asked me when e'er I cam in

A thocht they would drive me right owre the Linn;

Her - ding's the aul - dest trade of aa:

It be - gan way back o the year thir - ty twa

When he ge - thered the sheep frae the top o the glen

They wal - kit a - hint 'im right in - to the pen.

O when A was a laddie A leeved up a glen
A wis learning tae herd wi twae auld bearded men;
The questions they asked me when e'er I cam in,
A thocht they would drive me right owre the Linn.
Herding's the auldest trade of aa:
It began way back o the year thirty twa.
When he gethered the sheep frae the top o the glen
They walkit ahint 'im right into the pen.

But sheep have changed sair since A wis a lad,
There's mair hair than oo, an they arenae half clad.
In a cauld day in winter when raining or sleet
They crawl under moss haggs and no hunt for their meat.
Guid oo is essential upon a sheep's back;
Guid oo it is better when it is weel packed.
The oo cheque a shair yin the fermer's best whack,
An the sheets that are empty have aye tae gang back.

Unemployment in Scotland, thirty thoosand on the dole,
But they try tae tell ye its under control.
They would gie them aa scythes, put ten men in a beat
And gar them cut brackens and work for the meat.
The auld drainer he's deid and nae mair need be said,
But they hae said nowt about gaen 'em a spade,
Bogs are rotten wi rashies and spret that is laid,
Drains are full lying groaning, and needing first aid.

But hill ferming has changed tae a modern core,
The young say its better, the auld say its waur;
But needless tae say with their yowe ball galore
They'll no need a herd if they shout frae the door.
Yon auld herd and his plaidie you will ne'er see again
For they wear fancy plastics tae keep oot the rain;
And even the auld yowes in the top of the glen
In the winters wear a plaid, like yon auld bearded men.

In winterin hill yowes hae turned tae craze

They say they dae better than rinnin the braes.

A fermer wi money, can aye have a try

An grun tae gaun back on, like the Heid o the Dye;

This modern blackie must hae crashed wi a bang,

When she'll no stand the winter on the heft, where's she gaun?

Yon auld herd an guid hay was aye a safe plan,

An eichteen oot o twinty would aye rear a lamb.

'Gingling Geordie' winner of the President's medal and Borthwick
Challenge Cup, Hawick, and champion of Dumfries show. A mowhaugh
bred sheep owned by James McFarlane.

Fareweel Tae The Borders

Our native land - our native vale
A long an last adieu;
Fareweel tae bonnie Teviotdale,
And Cheviot's mountains blue.

Fareweel ye hills of glorious deeds,
And streams renown'd in song;
Fareweel ye blossom'd braes and meads,
Our hearts have loved so long.

Fareweel the blithsome broomie knowes,
Where thyme and harebells grow;
Fareweel the hoary haunted howes,
O'erhung with birk and sloe.

The mossy cave, the mouldering tower
That skirt our native dell;
The martyr's grave and lover's bower,
We bid a sad fareweel.

Home of our love - oor father's home,
Land of the brave and free;
The sail is flapping on the foam
That bears us far from thee.

We seek a wild and distant shore
Beyond the western main;
We leave thee to return no more,
Nor view thy cliffs again.

But may dishonour blight our fame,
And quench our household fire;
If we or ours forget thy fame,
Green island of our sires.

Our native land - our native vale
A long a last adieu;
Fareweel to bonnie Teviotdale
And Scotland's mountains blue.

My Ain Counterie

O the sun rises bright in France
And fair sits he:
But he has lost the look he had
In his ain counterie;
Gladness comes to many
As sorrow comes to me;
As I lookit owre the ocean wide
Tae my ain counterie.

It's no my ain guilt
That saddens aye my ee;
But the love I left in Galloway
Wi bonnie bairnies three.
A hamely hearth burns bonnie
As smiles my fair Mary,
But I left my heart behind me
In my ain counterie.

The bird comes back to summer
And the blossom to the tree;
But I cam back, o never
Tae my ain counterie.
A'm leal to high heaven
Which will aye be leal to me;
And I'll meet ye aa again soon
Frae my ain counterie.

Boys O Boys

♩.=96

O___ I've been a ser - vant lass___ This eigh - teen years and ten,___

I've spent all my life___ Up in Strath - du - ie___ Glen;___

But now I'm giv - ing it o - ver And I lift my six months pay,___

And I'm bound to say___ he'll bless the day___ the man that - 'll mar - ry mey.

chorus:

Boys,___ O boys,___ O won't you take a wife?

I'm sure ye can - na be hap - py lea - din a sin - gle life;___

Boys,___ O boys,___ get mair - ried while ye're young,___

And if its a ti - dy wee wife ye want___ Ye're eye - in the ve - ry one.

O I've been a servant lass
This eighteen years and ten,
I've spent all me life
Up in Strathduie Glen;
But now I'm giving it over
And I lift my six months pay,
And I'm bound to say he'll bless the day
The man that'll mairry mey.

Chorus
Boys, o boys,
O won't you take a wife?
I'm sure ye canna be happy
Leadin a single life;
Boys, o boys,
Get mairried while ye're young,
And if its a tidy wee wife ye want
Ye're eyein the very one.

I will keep his hoose both neat and clean
And everything complete,
And I will never give him cause
To ask his bargain back;
Instead o gien him a bowl o brose
I'll coax him up wi tey,
And I'm bound to say he'll bless the day
The man that'll mairry mey.

Chorus

I will put his children out tae school
I'm sure there will be two,
Ane ca'd for the mither
The ither yin ca'd for you;
And if good fortune smiles on me
I'm sure there must be three,
And I'm bound to say, he'll bless the day
The man that'll mairry mey.

Chorus

Now John leave off your gambling
And John leave off your frowns,
And when the term day comes round
Ye'll post me down your crowns;
And if ever you lift your hand John
Or use your foot to me,
I'm bound to say you'll rue the day
That ever you mairried mey.

Chorus

Nancy's Whisky

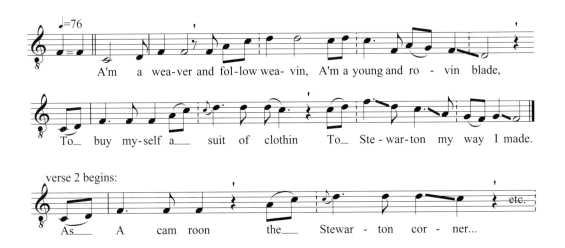

A'm a weaver and follow weavin, A'm a young and ro - vin blade,
To buy my-self a suit of clothin To Ste-war-ton my way I made.

verse 2 begins:

As A cam roon the Stewar - ton cor - ner... etc.

A'm a weaver and follow weavin,
A'm a young and rovin blade,
To buy myself a suit of clothin
To Stewarton my way I made.

As A cam roon the Stewarton corner
Nancy's whisky I did spy,
Says I tae masel, I'll gang in and taste her,
For seven lang years now A hae been dry.

Well the more A tasted, the more A liked it,
The more A tasted, A liked it more;
And the more A tasted, the more A liked it,
Til all my senses had gone ashore.

Twas early, early, the next morning,
A wakened in a stranger's bed,
A tried to rise but A was not able,
For Nancy's whisky held doon my head.

I called up to the landlady
And asked her what my reckoning was,
"Your reckoning is full thirty shillings
Come pay me quickly and go your way."

A put my hand in tae my pocket
And all A had A laid it doon;
And efter I had paid my reckoning
All A'd left was a poor half-croon.

As A came out and A turned the corner
A charming damsel A did spy,
On her A spent my two white shillings
And all A'd left was a crooked boy.

Noo A'll gang hame and A'll start the weaving,
And my wee shuttles A'll mak them fly;
And curses be on Nancy's whisky
For Nancy's whisky hae ruined I.

At Blairgowrie festival in 1967 with Davie Stewart, Bob Hobkirk and Bill Porter.

Callieburn

John Blair and I hae taen a notion
Tae cross the wide Atlantic ocean;
Rab MacKinlay's gaen afore us
He will keep us aa in order.

> *Chorus*
> Hame fareweel, freens fareweel
> And ye boys of Callieburn,
> Fare ye weel.

We leave the land of our forefathers
Knowing not what may befall us;
America, 'twas thee that wiled us
For to leave our aged parents.

> *Chorus*

Machrihanish, bright and bonnie,
O'er thy beach the waves are rolling;
Machrihanish I adore thee,
Never more I will be o'er thee.

> *Chorus*

We leave the land where we were born
And o, our parents won't disown us;
This is a song of our own composing
Comrades dear, come join the chorus.

> *Chorus*

O mother dear, I'm going to leave you
Knowing well it sorely grieves you;
But o mother dear, o do believe me
Till the day I die I'll ne'er deceive ye.

> *Chorus*

Bonnie Udny

Udny bonnie Udny ye shine where ye stand,
And the more I look on you it makes my heart warm:
For if I were in Udny, I would think myself at home
For there I have a true love, but here I have none.

Owre hills and through valleys I oft times have gone,
Through brambles and brushwood myself all alone;
Through hedges and ditches in dark nights and clear,
I hae wandered into Udny to visit my dear.

It's nae the lang journey that I hae to go,
It's nae the lang road that vexes me so;
It's the leaving o Udny and my loved one behind
O Udny, bonnie Udny, ye're aye in my mind.

Ae certain Sunday morning me and my love met,
Which caused me on the Monday to mourn o'er my fate;
To spoil my eyes crying, what a fool I would be,
For she's gone with another, go where will she.

Aa the young lads o Udny they're aa rovin blades,
They tak great delight in coortin fair maids;
They'll tak them and kiss them, and they'll spend their money free,
O places in bonnie Scotland, bonnie Udny for me.

Let's drink and be merry, let's drink and gang hame;
If we bide here muckle langer, we'll get a bad name:
We'll get a bad name, aye, and we'll fill oorsels fu,
And that lang road tae Udny we hae aye tae gang through.

With Daisy Chapman.

The Banks Of Inverurie

It was on a summer morning
Along as I did pass,
On the banks of Inverurie
I met a comely lass;
Her hair hung over her shoulders
Her eyes like stars did shine,
On the banks of Inverurie
I wish her heart was mine.

Now I did embrace this fair maid
As fast as e'er I could,
Her hair hung o'er her shoulders broad
All in its thread of gowd;
Her hair hung o'er her shoulders broad
And her eyes like drops of dew,
On the banks of Inverurie
I'm glad I've met with you.

"Leave off my handsome young man
Do not embrace me so,
For after so much kissing
There comes a dreadful woe;
And if my heart you ensnare
And you beguileth me,
On the banks of Inverurie
Alone I walk," says she.

I said "My pretty fair maid
The truth to you I'll tell,
On the banks of Inverurie
Twelve maidens I've beguiled;
But I'll not begin tonight
My charmer," said he
"On the banks of Inverurie
I've met my wife," said he.

Now he placed this pretty fair maid
On horseback very high,
And to a parson we will go
And there the knot we'll tie;
And we'll sing songs of love
Until the day we die,
On the banks of Inverurie
Where no one there is nigh.

Kissin In The Dark

♩.=92

Oh___ for lang A've cour-ted Jean-nie_ An A wrocht wi micht an main,

Tae hae a pi-ck-le sil-ler___ And a big-gin__ o me ain;

Ay___ nicht A gaed tae see her   Be it rain or mirk

A took her in ma airms___ aye And A kissed her in the dark.

chorus:

O the dark,___ the dark,___ the dark, the dark, the dark,___

A took her in ma airms__ aye, And A kissed her in the dark.___

Willie Scott, Jimmy MacBeath and Davie Stewart at a TMSA Festival.

Oh for lang A've courted Jeannie
An A wrocht wi micht and main,
Tae hae a pickle siller
And a biggin o me ain;
Ay nicht A gaed tae see her
Be it rain or mirk,
A took her in my airms aye
And A kissed her in the dark.

Chorus
O the dark, the dark,
The dark, the dark, the dark,
A took her in ma airms aye,
And A kissed her in the dark.

Yin nicht A gaed tae see her,
And my Jeannie wis frae hame;
A tiptoed tae the window
And A rattled on the pain:
Oot cam Jeannie's mither
The nicht it being sae dark,
A took her in ma airms aye,
And A kissed her in the dark.

Chorus

She huggit and she tuggit,
An she thocht she'd won awa;
A held her aye the closer
An A gied her ither twa;
She bursted oot a-laughin
An says it's awfu wark,
To tousle an auld body aye,
An kiss her in the dark.

Chorus

Noo we hadnae lang been married
When Jeannie's mither she took ill,
She sent me for a lawyer
She wis gaun tae mak her will;
She left me all her siller
Efter aa ma courtin wark,
An A got the auld wife's blessin
For the kissin in the dark.

Chorus

The Banks Of Newfoundland

air: Come aa ye tramps and hawkers

Come all ye men and young lads and sportsmen be aware
If you go steamboat sailing a dungaree jacket wear;
And always wear a life belt or have one close at hand
For cold blows the cold nor-westerly winds on the banks of Newfoundland.

We had some passengers on board some Swedies and some more;
It was the year nineteen hundred and six that we did suffer sore.
We pawned our clothes in Liverpool, we pawned them every hand
And forgot the cold nor-westerly winds on the banks of Newfoundland.

We had a fair maid on board, Bridget Wellwood was her name,
To her I promised marriage, on me she had a claim;
She tore her flannel petticoats to make mittens for my hands,
For she could not see her true love perish on the banks of Newfoundland.

Last night as I lay upon my bed I dreamt a beautiful dream,
I dreamt I was home in Scotland beside a running stream;
My true love she sat on my knee, I'd a bottle in my hand
But I woke up broken-hearted on the banks of Newfoundland.

But now we're off for Hudson Bay we'll get there in a day,
Our steam goes at half a pass by New York we will go.
We'll rub her up and scrub her down with holy-stone and sand,
And we'll bid farewell to the virgin rocks on the banks of Newfoundland.

Willie singing at the Sydney Opera House with his son, Sandy.

Song Of The Gillie More

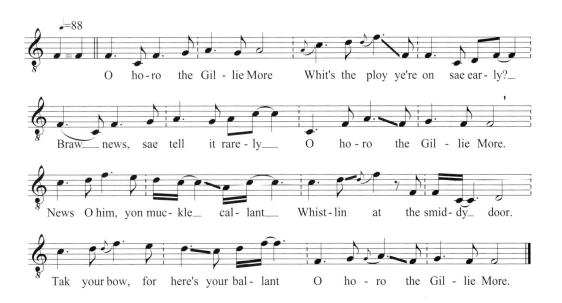

O horo the Gillie More

Whit's the ploy ye're on sae early?

Braw news, sae tell it rarely

O horo the Gillie More.

News o' him, yon muckle callant

Whistlin at the smiddy door.

Tak your bow, for here's your ballant

O horo the Gillie More.

O horo the Gillie More

Come awa an gie's your blether.

Here's a dram'll droon the weather

O horo the Gillie More.

Sons o birk an pine an rowan

Jocks and Ivans by the score

Swappin yarns tae cowe the gowan

O horo the Gillie More.

O horo the Gillie More

Noo's the time, the haimmer's ready.

Haud the tangs - ay, haud them steady

O horo the Gillie More.

Gar the iron ring, avallich!

Gar it ring frae shore tae shore.

Leith tae Kiev - Don tae Gairloch

O horo the Gillie More.

O horo the Gillie More

Here's a weld'll wear for ever.

Oor grup they canna sever

O horo the Gillie More.

Ane's the wish yokes us thegither -

Ane's the darg that lies afore.

You an me: the man, the brither!

Me an you: the Gillie More.

In Freenship's Name

Here a - roon the in - gle bleez - in'

Whae sae hap - py and sae free,

Though the nor - thern winds blaw free - zy

Freen - ship warms baith you and me.

chorus: [steady]

Hap - py we've been aa the - gi - ther

Can - ty we've been yin and aa,

Time shall see us aa mair bli - ther

Ere we rise tae gang a - wa.

Here aroon the ingle bleezin
Whae sae happy and sae free,
Though the northern winds blaw freezy
Freenship warms baith you and me.

Chorus
    Happy we've been aa thegither
    Canty we've been yin and aa;
    Time shall see us aa mair blither
    Ere we rise tae gang awa.

See the miser owre his treisure
Glutton wi a greedy ee,
Wha can fill his woes wi pleisure
As aroond us here we see.

Chorus

Can the peer in silk and ermine
Caa his conscience half his ain,
His claes are edged and spun with vermine
Though he sits upon a throne.

Chorus

Thus then let us aa be tassin
Though owre the stoops o generous fame;
And while roon the board is passin
Raise a sang in freenship's name.

Chorus

Freenship maks us aa mair happy,
Freenship gies us a delight;
Freenship consecrates the drappie,
Freenship brocht us here the night.

Chorus

SONG NOTES
by
Geordie McIntyre

James and Ellen Scott with their family.(backrow) Willie, Mat, Tom, Jock and Sandy; (seated) Cis and Nell.
Taken about 1916.

In the Notes the following names and abbreviations have been used to indicate the origin of the material:

MOSB	**Minstrelsy of the Scottish Borders** collected by Sir Walter Scott; first edition (1802) Kelso Press followed by countless reprints
RC	**Songs of Scotland (Prior to Burns)** ed. Robert Chambers Edinburgh (1862) pub: W.R. Chambers
LG	**Lyric Gems of Scotland** first and second series Glasgow (1856) pub: John Cameron
SM	**Scottish Minstrel** (songs and songwriters subsequent to Burns) Edinburgh (1885)
FORD	**Vagabond Songs and Ballads of Scotland** ed. Robert Ford Paisley (1904) pub: Alex Gardner
ORD	**Ord's Bothy Songs and Ballads** collected/edited by John Ord Paisley (1930) pub: Alex Gardner, new edition, Edinburgh (1990) pub: John Donald
DICK	**The Songs of Robert Burns** ed. James C Dick Facsimile of 1903 edition (Newcastle) Folklore Associates, Hatboro, Pennysylvania (1962) pub. Folklore Associates
CHILD	**The English and Scottish Popular Ballads** ed.Francis James Child, 5 volumes, Boston (1882-98), new edition, New York, pub: Dover Books (2005)
G/D	**The Greig-Duncan Folk Song Collection** (8 volumes) ed. EB Lyle, P. Shuldham Shaw et. al., University of Aberdeen, published 1981 to 2002 (Vols 1 to 4 Aberdeen University Press; Vols 5-8 Mercat Press)
TOCHER	**Tocher (Tales/Songs/Tradition)** selected from archives of the School of Scottish and Celtic Studies, Edinburgh University No 25 (1977), No 31 (1979)
PALMER	**Boxing the Compass: Sea Songs and Chanties** ed. Roy Palmer Herron Pub. (2001)
SHEPARD	**The Broadside Ballad** by Leslie Shepard Reprint of 1962 edition by E.P. publishers Wakefield, Yorkshire (1978)
SH	**Sam Henry's Songs of the People** ed. Gayle Huntington University of Georgia Press (1990)
KIDSON	**Traditional Tunes** ed. Frank Kidson (1891): facsimile reprint (1999)
SMM	**The Scots Musical Museum** (1787-1803) ed. James Johnson and Robert Burns; new edition, Aldershot, Scolar Press (1991)
WHITELAW	**The Book of Scottish Song** ed. Alexander Whitelaw, Glasgow (1844)

SWEET COPSHAWHOLM

From the pen of James Telfer an ancestor of Willie. Copshawholm is the old name for Newcastleton, a place and area very dear to him. There has been an annual traditional music festival in 'Copshie' since the 1960's. A kenspeckle figure and regular guest performer was of course, Willie.

THE SOFT LOWLAND TONGUE O THE BORDERS

Written and composed by William Sanderson (1853-1945) a journalist and poet. As a poet he wrote under the name of 'Tweedside Laddie' and for many years edited the Border Magazine. It is often sung at Border Common Ridings and has been recorded over the years by such performers as Robert Wilson and later by Moira Anderson and Peter Mallan.

Thanks to Henry Douglas of Bonchester Bridge for extra information.

COPSHAWHOLM FAIR

This sprightly and spirited narrative was collected by Frank Kidson (1855-1926) at Gilknockie in Dumfrieshire. (see Kidson: page 98) Willie sings a fuller text and it was in fact from the pen of a local man, David Anderson ,written in 1838. The song was also in the repertoire of the late Dick Cowan of Liddesdale.

WHEN THE KYE CAMS HAME

The editor of LG described this as "the most popular of all the Ettrick shepherd's songs". It was written by James Hogg and first appeared in his novel "The Three Perils of Man".

TWAS ON YIN NIGHT IN SWEET JULY

Better known as *The Brundenlaws*, which is a farm lying close to Jeddart (Jedburgh). The late Francis Collinson, collecting on behalf of the then recently formed School of Scottish Studies, recorded an almost identical version from James Cockburn of Kelso in 1952.

THE DOWIE DENS O YARROW (Child 214)

A widespread , classic ballad which was first printed in MOSB and in Scott's own words was, "universally believed to be founded in fact". The dramatic storyline and its sheer poignancy all contributed to its enduring popularity. This version, among many, is of high poetic and musical merit. It is one of the most famous of all the Border Ballads.

WHEN FORTUNE TURNS HER WHEEL

A song which circulated widely in broadside format emanating from the like of the famous 'Poet's Box' in Glasgow. The Mitchell Library in Glasgow has become an important repository of such material.

PULLING HARD AGAINST THE STREAM

This is from the pen of Harry Clifton (1824-72), a remarkable English music hall performer who wrote over 500 songs, perhaps the best known being, *Pretty Polly Perkings of Paddington Green*. Clifton wrote many songs which have entered the repertoire of traditional singers, e.g. *On Board The Kangaroo*, sung by the late Bess Cronin of Macroom in County Cork and *The Watercress Girl*, sung by the late Tommy Morrisey of Padstow in Cornwall. This particular song is one of the so called 'motto' type which have a strong moralistic tone. Many thanks to Steve Gardham for his expert help with this note.

JIMMIE RAEBURN

A transportation ballad that was highly popular and gained wide circulation via chapbooks and broadsides. In County Donegal its title was changed to Jimmy Leeburn, but the story is the same. It appears as song No1535 in G/D.

TIME WEARS AWA

This text, to a quite different tune, appears in LG: second series, p276. It is from the pen of Fermanagh born Thomas Elliot, of Border descent. It is highly probable that this book source was in the Scott household.

COME AA YE TRAMPS AND HAWKERS

This 'on-the-road' song is attributed to Besom Jimmy, an Angus hawker, and is of relatively recent origin, circa 1900. Various versions exist including 'Tramps and Navvies' from Mary Brooksbank of Dundee.

TINKER'S WADDIN

A song that has entered the "carrying stream" of oral tradition and is widely distributed in Scotland. It is from the pen of William Watt of West Linton, Peebleshire (1792-1859). Ford describes it as 'a classic of its kind, humorous, graphic and rattling'.

LOCK THE DOOR LARISTON

Perhaps the epitome of Border feud ballads, this is from the prolific pen of James Hogg (1770-1835) better known as The Ettrick Shepherd: see LG, first series, p69.

HERMITAGE CASTLE

This stark edifice and monument to battle ghosts has been well described as "a vast eery fortress at the heart of many of the bloodiest events in the history of the Borders".

THERE'S BOUND TO BE A ROW

This is on a well-worked theme and dates from circa 1870.The text appeared on broadsides and has, clearly, travelled.Very similar versions were sung by the late Jimmy McBeath of Banffshire and Harry Cox of Norfolk. Both of these fine singers, like Willie, took great delight in its rendition! GD,vol 7 no:12817.

JOHNNY RAW

Appears in ORD (p395) without a tune and is titled *I Wish My Granny Saw Ye*. The theme of the country man experiencing various forms of misfortune in the city is well worked, reflected in such songs as *Jock Hawk's Adventures in Glasgow*.

DONALD'S RETURN TO GLENCOE

This song, and song type, had wide circulation and popularity. It is in the 'broken-token' category however the usual half-ring is replaced with a glove in this version. Sam Henry collected a fine example, minus the mythological allusions, in Coleraine in the 1930's to its other title *The Pride of Glencoe*: SH, p319.

THE BAND O SHEARERS

Enjoying widespread circulation, Grieg-Duncan has no less than eight version (G/D song No 406). Ford attributes the song to Robert Hogg, nephew of the Ettrick Shepherd. This is contentious but I'm sure many Borderers will concur with Ford!

JAMIE TELFER O THE FAIR DODHEID (Child 190)

A very rare and valuable fragment of a classic Border riding-ballad which Willie learned from his mother. Hamish Henderson informs us "it is the first tune ever to be recorded for this ballad". This gem can be heard on The Muckle Sangs vol 5, (See Discography).

GREEN GROWS THE LAURELS

Widespread and popular in oral and print traditions, versions have been recorded in Ireland (its possible origin) Scotland, England and North America. Laurel represents innocence and fickleness in colour symbolism. This version is, atypically, from the male viewpoint. Willie omits the important last verse. A sample of such is:

> Now I often do wonder why young men love maids
>
> And I often do wonder why young maids love men
>
> But by my experience well I ought to know
>
> Young maids are deceivers wherever they go

THE WILD COLONIAL BOY

One of the best-known Australian folk songs with numerous variants set to a range of tunes. Sam Henry published a fine version, worthy of comparison with Willie's and points out that Jack's birthplace is in Co Kerry. It had wide distribution in broadside form (SH p120).

THE LADS THAT WERE REARED AMANG HEATHER

This is believed to have originated in Dumfrieshire. It was also quite common in Peebleshire around the turn of the twentieth century.

BLOODY WATERLOO

A large number of songs about Napoleon and Waterloo have survived in the tradition. This is an uncommon 'soldier's return' song which is closely related in story line to the widespread and better known, *Banks of Claudy*.

SONS O BONNIE SCOTLAND

Adam MacNaughton has come to my rescue with this one and informs me that it is from the pen of Scottish Music Hall artiste and composer, Alec Melville, who, incidentally, wrote songs for Harry Lauder. Songs of this nature and sentiment circulated in great quantity but often never appeared in print. However, this was printed in one of the numerous, popular and cheap song booklets, without music, published by Felix McGlennon of Liverpool. Such products were in a direct line from the earlier chapbooks.

THE SOLDIER'S RETURN

A genuine squaddie song from the trenches, which in its own way, brings to my mind the classic soldier's song, *Westron Wynde*.

> Westron wynde when will thou blow?
>
> The small rain down doth rain
>
> Christ, that my love was in my arms
>
> And I in my bed again

THE WAG AT THE WAA

A relatively modern song with a distinct music-hall ring to it. It may well be of North-East origin, since the source of the song, John Galbraith and Willie's brother Tom were in the Gordon Highlanders! In addition, Peter Hall of Aberdeen collected a version from traditional singer Lottie Buchan.

OWRE THE MUIR AMANG THE HEATHER

This fine song appears as No 328 in the SMM and was contributed by Burns who collected it from the singing of Jean Glover of Kilmarnock. Burns asserted that she was also the authoress. Willie' version is slightly shorter and bears clear hallmarks of oral transmission. This pastoral theme and encounter is a familiar one in the Scots and Irish song tradition reflected in such handsome and distinctive versions as *Queen Amang The Heather* and *Doon The Moor*: see S H page 271.

THE BONNIE WEE TRAMPIN LASS

A song which may well be of Northern Irish origin. Sam Henry collected a fine *The Bonny Wee Lass* in Carrickfergus (see SH p458) and other versions, describing it as 'widely known'. Gavin Greig suggested it was from the southwest of Scotland and given the 'ten bob' reference "relatively modern" (G/D no 1917).

MISTRESS PAXTON'S SHOP

Shops of this type, "Jenny Aa Things," stocking a wide variety of goods were once common. Sandy Scott, Willie's son, has suggested that the location of this particular one may have been in Smailholm, Roxburghshire, prior to 1900.

THE SHEPHERD'S SONG

From the singing of John Irvine of Langholm via Willie's brother, Tom although he first heard old Willie Graham sing it. This was surely Willie's signature-tune since it reflects so much of his own life in fifty two years of herding.

LAMBING TIME

This descriptive piece seems to be of Borders origin and was learnt by Willie around 1947.

DANDIE

A little cameo of a shepherd and his dog, this was evidently a great favourite at verse-speaking festivals. It is from the prolific pen of Glasgow born vernacular poet W.D. Cocker (1882-1970)

THE WADDIN O McPHEE

One of the many parodies of the very familiar *Bonnie Banks of Loch Lomond* , sung to the standard tune, which, incidentally, was collected by Lady John Scott (1811-1900). She also wrote her own version of the older song which, in tradition, was spoken by a Jacobite soldier about to be hung at Carlisle. Willie enjoyed parodies and indeed had yet another version in his handwritten collection.

THE TIME O YEAR FOR DIPPIN SHEEP

From the pen of Buff Wilson of Irvine, Ayrshire and learned by Willie in the 1960's.

AN AWFA CHAP FOR FUN

Echoes of the Music Hall abound in this witty, pacey lyric.

PIPER MacNEIL

Learned from Wull Scott, a shepherd who was also a piper and fiddler who worked at Eskdalemuir, Dumfrieshire just prior to World War 1.

MY HIELAN HAME

A copy of this text appears in Broadside format, printed in Glasgow by Robert McIntosh, titled "My Hielan Hame". The date of publication is probably circa 1880.

THE YELLA HAIRED LADDIE

From the pen of Thomas C Latto, born at Kingsbarns in Fife, 1818. It first appeared in print without music in WHITELAW. Willie set his own tune to it. Thanks to singer/songwriter Adam MacNaughtan for help with this one.

BONNIE JEANNIE SHAW

A fine, albeit much reduced, version of the original composition by Alexander Melville (see ORD p344). In Willie's way of it, Cathkin Braes, south of Glasgow, becomes the Calpin Braes.

JOHN REILLY

From the pen of Edward (Ned) Harrigan, written in 1881. Harringan was part of the legendary duo of Harrigan and Hart "the idols of vaudeville and theatre" in the late 1800's in New York. I first heard this song among the cycling and outdoor (climbing) fraternity, where versions are still sung. The original has 4 verses and a chorus, so Willie's way of it is incomplete; verse 4 of the original is printed below:

What puzzles all the doctors

John Reilly ever met

Is fresh or salty water

Can't make John Reilly wet

Sure he must have the liquor,

Raum, brandy gin or rye.

And Should he miss the bottle, boys

John Reilly surely would die

Thanks to Jim and Joan Brown for help, providing their "climber's" version.

JOCK GEDDES AND THE SOO

There are many songs dealing with the dangers of whisky taken to excess. This is one of the more light hearted ones. Its first appearance in print was, allegedly as a prize song in the People's Friend. The fine tune is a variant of *Roy's Wife of Aldivalloch*.

SCOTCH MEDLEY

This appears as a broadside ballad dated between 1880-1900 from the renowned "Poet's Box" in Dundee. There were similar 'Poet's Boxes' in Glasgow, Edinburgh, Paisley, Belfast and elsewhere. The significance of broadsides and chapbooks as song sources, as well as their co-existence and interaction with oral tradition should be recognised.

> "originally perpetuated by word of mouth many ballads survive because they were recorded as broadsides. Musical notation was rarely printed, as tunes were usually established favourites. The term "ballad" applied broadly to any kind of topical or popular verse"

KILLIEBANK BRAES

There are numerous examples of songs of this pastoral nature and romantic theme, however this is my first acquaintance with a feisty shepherdess such as the finale reveals. It is evidently a local song.

BONNY TYNESIDE

A Northumberland song from the pen of George Chapp of Wall near Hexham. It is typical of the exile wanderer's return variety. The last verse may not be realistic – but it is certainly romantic.

THE KIELDER HUNT

A Northumbrian song written by James Armstrong of Redesdale and which dates from the late nineteenth century. It has established itself on both sides of the Border.

THE DROUTHIE DRIVER

I am unable to trace the author, however it is clearly inspired, in both rhythm and character, by Burns's famous *Tam O'Shanter*. Willie had a strong liking for songs and poems with a moral, especially if infused with humour. This poem fits the bill on both counts.

MACALISTER DANCES BEFORE THE KING

It was a privilege to hear Willie deliver this famous recitation-piece from the pen of D. M. MacKenzie. It was believed to be a favourite of the late Queen Elizabeth, the Queen Mother.

IRTHINGWATER FOXHOUNDS

Songs of hunting, as distinct from poaching, are uncommon in the oral tradition. This rarity is from the North of England. The River Irthing lies close to Brampton in Cumbria, to the South of Liddesdale.

THE CANNY SHEPHERD LADDIE O THE HILLS

Hannah Hutton of Rothbury, Northumberland, infoms me that this is from the pen of Jack Mowat, a travelling draper from Rothbury. A version, close to Willie's way of it, was collected by Peter Kennedy in 1954 from Jimmy White of Yetlington, Northumberland, set to the same well known air, *Keep Your Feet Still Geordie Hinny*.

HERD LADDIE O THE GLEN

Willie's skill as a versifier is well demonstrated here. An enduring theme is the chronicling of change and lament for the passing of old ways. Here it is tackled with typical humour and insight born of knowledge and hard-won experience. It was written as a tribute to an old friend and set to the air of *Bonny Strathyre*.

FAREWELL TAE THE BORDERS

An emigration poem, typical of its kind, with a handsome tune set by Willie.

MY AIN COUNTERIE

This is a version of *The Sun Rises Bright In France* and in its original form was composed by Allan Cunningham (1784-1842) born in Dalswinton in Dumfrieshire. His father was a friend of Robert Burns. Allan, aged twelve, attended the poet's funeral in 1796 and later became a friend of James Hogg and Walter Scott.

BOYS O BOYS

The 1979 edition, No 31 of Tocher has a major feature by Hamish Henderson on the famed Mitchell family of Kintyre. The source for this song was the late Willie Mitchell, local bard and song-collector and we are informed that this "was the first song from Kintyre oral tradition" which Willie Mitchell recorded in his songbook as "Oh Boys Oh".

NANCY'S WHISKY

Clearly, in text and distinctive tune, a Kintyre version of the widely known *Dublin Weaver* or *Calton Weaver*. The Stewarton referred to is a village close to Campbelltown. It is, once again, from the singing of Willie Mitchell (TOCHER, No31 and G/D song No 603).

CALLIEBURN

After the event, Willie often said "I never kent a man like that existed" referring to kindred spirit Willie Mitchell of Kintyre. The event being the fabled impromptu ceilidh at Blairgowrie in 1968. Willie was 'bowled over' by this poignant, distinctive emigration song delivered by the singing-butcher, so much so, he learned it that very night (TOCHER No. 25, 1977)

BONNIE UDNY

This is song No 1984 in G/D and there are nineteen versions and variants therein. Although localised, Grieg notes it is not necessarily of Aberdeenshire origin since we have versions titled: *Bonnie Portrush, Bonnie Kilkenny, Bonnie Yarmouth* and *Bonnie Paisley*. Its origin may be in doubt but not its widespread popularity! In short, typical localisation of a good song has occurred.

THE BANKS OF INVERURIE

There are six versions of this Northeast-rooted song in G/D. Learned from Daisy Chapman, the text is very close to the "B" version, in G/D, song no. 1263.

KISSIN IN THE DARK

Another from Daisy Chapman which is less complete than that printed in ORD, however, the gist of this witty narrative is not lost. It was recorded in the 1960's by John Mearns, another noted Aberdeenshire singer of bothy songs.

THE BANKS OF NEWFOUNDLAND

Older versions, i.e. 19th century, of this fine maritime song, of the forebitter type, paint a graphic picture of a hard western-ocean crossing before the days of steam. Willie's version is distinctive in various ways: in terms of tune *Tramps and Hawkers*, absence of the more usual chorus and we are now in the age of steam (1906). Widespread in oral tradition and via broadsides, it was printed by Ross of Newcastle around 1850.

SONG OF THE GILLIE MORE

This song dates from 1948 and was written by Hamish Henderson (1919-2002). Inspired by a Scottish-Soviet Friendship Week where "fraternal good wishes were exchanged between the Blacksmiths of Leith and the Blacksmiths of Kiev". Willie learned the song much later and, no doubt, its fusion of Burnsian egalitarianism and its celebration of working-folk solidarity was well in tune with his own firm philosophy.

IN FREENSHIP'S NAME

This appears in LG, series 2, p229, as *Here Around the Ingle Bleezin* with four verses and chorus. Willie has an extra verse, verse 3. This delightful convivial song cannot be bettered for quality and sentiment and is a most appropriate song to close this collection.

DISCOGRAPHY

The Borders: Songs And Dances Of The English-Scottish Border

Willie Scott with members of his family and others

Folkways Records (USA) FW8776 (1960)

The Shepherd's Song: Willie Scott

Re-Issue Of 1968 Topic Records, L.P. Greentrax Recordings, East Lothian; Scotland

CDtrax 9054 (1998)

The Voice Of The People

CD series Topic Records London

A selection of tracks taken from the original record and recordings by Bill Leader, included in this 20 volume themed series, i.e. TSCD670 'There Is A Man Upon The Farm, working men and women in song'

The Muckle Sangs: Classic Scots Ballads

Willie sings *Jamie Telfer* fragment

CD Re-Issue of Tangent Records TNGM 119/D by Greentrax: CDtrax 9005

Borders Sangsters

Willie Scott et al: Willie Sings:

> *Piper McNeill*
>
> *There's Bound To Be A Row*
>
> *The Shepherd's Song*
>
> *The Kielder Hunt*

Living Tradition, Kilmarnock, Scotland and Scottish Borders Council

LTCD002 (2002)

GLOSSARY

A

aa	all
ae	one
abuin	above
ane	one
arles	engage for service by paying sum of money
avallich	my lad, from Gaelic, a bhalaich

B

ballant	ballad
be	by
bey	be
biggin	building, cottage
birk	birch
blackin	stove cleaner
blaw	brag, boast
blether(in)	to talk, idle chatter
blithe	joyous, happy
board	table
bowsie	puffed up
braes	hills
braw	fine
braxy	the salted flesh of a diseased sheep
brackens	ferns
bucht	pen for ewes at weaning time
burgonet	a plumed metal helmet

C

callants	lads
canny	clever, careful, wise, dextrous
canty	brisk, smart
cauler jeel	fresh or cold jelly
chaffed	chatted
chappin	clock striking
chiel	fellow, young man
coothie	friendly, sociable

coronach	funeral lament
cowe the gowan	beat all
crooked boy	small unusable coin
cushats	pigeon or dove
cut	to castrate male lambs
cyair	cure

D

darg	work, toil
dams	dames
daunerin	strolling
dens	narrow valleys
dod	god
dole	to be unemployed
drouth	thirst
dyke	wall

E

eident	busy
ellie	to idle away, walk away in a relaxed manner
elshun hefts	awl handles

F

fank	sheep pen
foumart	polecat
fu frig	primped up
fu	full of alcohol, i.e. drunk

G

galace	braces
gar	to make
gemlicks	gimlets
gillie more	big fellow
glamourie	magic, enchantment
glar	muddy, dirty
gloamin	twilight, dusk
glowerin	to stare intensely
gowans	daisies
gowdies	Gouda cheese

gravat	cravat or scarf
gundy	toffee

H

hads	a hole or place of retreat
hags	a hillock of firmer ground
hail	whole
haud yer wheesht	keep silent
heft	an accustomed pasture
hirsel	care of a flock of sheep in a given area
howes	a hollow or low lying piece of ground

I

ingle	fireside

K

keely	pencils
knowes	knolls
kye	cattle

L

laich	low
laiverock	the skylark
leal	loyal, faithful
leish	athletic, supple
loons	young lads/boys

M

mairlan	moorland
mawkit	sheep with maggots, Border shepherds also refer to 'mackit' sheep
mauna	must not
marrow	equal
merk	to mark and show ownership
mirk	dark
muckle	large, great, much
mowdies	moles

N

nebcloot	a type of nail
noddle	head
nook	corner, place

O

oo	wool
oor	hour

P

parrocking	getting a ewe to accept another ewe's lamb by confining them to gather in a small enclosure or paddock.
paunches	the entrails of an animal especially as used for food; tripe
pether	a pedlar or packman
pickle	a small or indefinite amount
plisky	trick
ploy	venture
preens	pins
prigs	begs

R

randie	rascal

S

sheuch	trench, drain
sheiling	high or remote summer pasture
siccan	such
skealin	scaling/climbing
slack	slow
slap	gate or wall-gap
smiddy	a blacksmiths shop
sole	windowsill
sparrables	flat nails for soles of shoes
spean	to separate the lamb from its mother
speywife	female fortune teller
speir	to ask, to inquire
spree	innocent, boisterous merriment
spret	a coarse reedy rush or grass growing on marshy ground
sugarallie	a liquorice stick confection
sweir	unwilling, reluctant

T

tassin	drinking
thrawcrairs	hooks for twisting ropes

thrawn	stubborn
thoule	to endure or suffer
tinker	itinerant pedlar or tinsmith; has taken on pejorative meaning, the modern acceptable term is now "traveller".
trig	active, nimble, alert
twinning	getting a stronger ewe to take a second lamb along with her own, sometimes helped by tying on the skin of a ewe's own dead lamb (i.e. cheat them with a skin)
tyke	dog

U

udderlock	gently pulling wool off the udder for the lamb to suck

W

wag-at-the-waa	an unencased, pendulum wall clock
wammle	roll
wezans	windpip
whaup	curlew
wheen	a small number
whings	bootlaces
wot	I must say, become aware of, I do believe
wrocht	to work
wyce	shrewd, knowing

Y

yauld	active, alert, vigorous
yaisual	usual, soon
yett	gate
yowe	ewe
yill	ale

Main sources:

Sandy Scott of St Boswells, Roxburghshire

THE CONCISE SCOTTISH DICTIONARY editor Mairi Robinson Aberdeen University Press (1985) edition

JAMIESON'S DICTIONARY OF THE SCOTTISH LANGUAGE (abridged) Edinburgh, William P Nimmo (1867)

song index